7 Steps to a Language-Rich Interactive Classroom

RESEARCH-BASED STRATEGIES FOR ENGAGING ALL STUDENTS

John Seidlitz
and Bill Perryman

Published by Seidlitz Education
56 Via Regalo
San Clemente, CA 92673
www.seidlitzeducation.com

To obtain permission to use material from this work, please submit a written
request to Seidlitz Education Permissions Department, 56 Via Regalo, San
Clemente, CA 92673

For related titles and support materials visit www.seidlitzeducation.com.

ACKNOWLEDGEMENTS

First and foremost, it is important to express our thanks to the many skilled educators in the Floresville ISD and the Northeast ISD in San Antonio, Texas. We thank all of the administrators and teachers who provided numerous opportunities to work and learn with them and from them. We are especially grateful for the support and learning opportunities provided by Deborah Short and her colleagues, Jana Echevarria and Mary Ellen Vogt. We are also grateful for the feedback and support provided by Melissa Castillo. Her unique educational approach to English Language Learner methodology was meaningful, important, and valuable.

We owe a great deal of gratitude to the staff at Seidlitz Education. Nancy Motley and Cindy Jones worked tirelessly on this research-based book to make sure it was both teacher-friendly and student-friendly. We would also like to thank Mónica Lara, Marguerite Hartill, Valerie Auer, Anne-Charlotte Patterson, Kathy Belanger, and Michelle Belanger for their feedback and support.

We are deeply grateful to Angel Torres, Bridgette Vieh, and other educators in the McAllen ISD for allowing us to use the Seven Steps with their teachers as a model for school improvement. We are also grateful to Paula Camacho, Bel Sanchez, and Jennifer Greer from the Alvin ISD; Tessie Young, Elva Conrardy, and Jim Hallamek from the Bastrop ISD; and Eric McGarrah and Marie Mendoza from the Northeast ISD. We must also acknowledge the Texas Education Agency and the Regional Education Service Centers across Texas, especially Region 20 and Region 13, for all the knowledge and information they have shared.

We are genuinely thankful and indebted to Alma Seidlitz for her outstanding ideas and her support throughout the creation of this book. We are especially appreciative of her tender care of Theresa, Gabriel, John Paul, Anna, and Peter Seidlitz. With their love, patience, and willingness to endure time apart from Daddy, this resource book was written and many teachers were trained to use it in the classroom.

Finally, we wish to thank God who provides real meaning and direction in our lives. As we work together, we give kids across the United States the gift of academic language.

TABLE OF contents

PART 2
READING AND WRITING
ACTIVITIES that support Steps 6 & 7 with a Twist!...62

APPENDIX 1

APPENDIX 2

APPENDIX 3

APPENDIX 4

BIBLIOGRAPHY

INTRODUCTION

By Bill Perryman

Sixth grade was not my favorite year in elementary school. When I entered my homeroom class on the first day of the school year, I noticed mountains of worksheets standing tall at the back of the room. They were an omen for what was to come.

In sixth grade, we changed classes for our core subjects every day, but each classroom looked the same, with desks in straight rows in front of the teacher's desk. Interaction among students was non-existent, except when we finished our assignments and had a chance to visit with one another. Class dynamics and participation were similar with every instructor. The teacher would call on one student at a time while the rest of us zoned out, patiently waiting for that one lone response.

In science class, we took notes all year long but did few, if any, experiments. In English class, we labored through a boring and complicated workbook until I almost felt illiterate! And math was a complete disaster. One month, the teacher stopped teaching math to have us research famous mathematicians. This exercise turned into, you guessed it... a written report. Social Studies class was no better. Remember that mountain of worksheets at the back of the room? We climbed that mountain for one whole year.

But things were about to change. Fast-forward a few years to my high school biology teacher, Ms. Conrads. She was a great teacher, passionate about science and teaching. She provided an interactive, "hands-on" classroom with engaging and fun lessons. In her classroom, we worked in groups to complete actual experiments. Ms. Conrads helped us learn science in a way that made sense. In fact, her lessons will be with me for the rest of my life. With Ms. Conrads, I experienced the best of teaching: engagement, higher-level thinking, a warm, safe environment, and a passionate delivery of the content.

As a teenager, I liked Ms. Conrads because her class was engaging and fun. As I studied educational methods over the years, I now understand why she was so successful. The way Ms. Conrads taught matched the way our brains learn. Many years later, her teaching methods would come to be supported by scientific research. The impact of this research is ground-breaking, and the implications of science on education are invaluable. For teachers, it means that we can tailor education to meet student needs. This sounds like a simple concept, but it has been a long time in the making. Ms. Conrads might be honored to find that she was on the cutting-edge of education so many years ago.

With these findings from the most current scientific research, we know that we need to get students to stand, move, and share their knowledge with one another. We need to provide adequate time for reflection. We need to add novelty and excitement to our lessons. And, we need to teach students the learning strategies that will help them find success in the real world. But are we hearing the message? A recent study of 1,500 American classrooms (Schmoker, 2006) produced startling data. It showed that in 85% of the classrooms, less than half of the students were paying attention. Only 3% of the classrooms showed evidence of higher-thinking activities, and over half of the lessons focused primarily on worksheets.

The leading problem with worksheet "drill and kill" education is its negative effect on students. These exercises convince kids that school is not a place where they want to be. Instead of drill and kill exercises, instruction needs to be creative, filled with positive emotion, and it needs to challenge young minds. According to a study conducted by the BBC, the ability to read well is the **single best indicator** of future economic success, regardless of family background (Schmoker, 2006). When students become literate and articulate, they will enjoy learning, and they will succeed.

Literacy, however, is more than just reading words on a page. It also includes the ability to engage students in meaningful conversations and to have them write with power and purpose in authentic situations. Educational researchers are increasingly paying attention to the significance of classroom discussion and the relationship to literacy (Graff, 2003; Rose, 1989).

Literacy is paramount in the quest for an educated citizenry in a democratic society. It is the ticket to success and upward mobility. When we prepare students to speak and write coherently, we are preparing them to be successful in life.

As a teacher and an educational consultant, I have begun to see the importance of *argumentative literacy*. While I have always worked to foster a learning atmosphere in which students are actively engaged, focusing on argumentative literacy adds another dimension of purpose and mission to my teaching.

Argumentative literacy could be described as the ability of an individual to engage in a coherent discussion, to articulate ideas, and to defend or support an idea or issue intelligently with breadth and depth. This includes the ability to step inside someone else's shoes and to see things from their perspective, a trait that is foreign to many students (Wiggins & McTighe, 1998).

A few years ago, I began working with John Seidlitz, and I quickly learned that we shared a passion for the art of teaching. John was as passionate about academic literacy as I was about meaningful student interaction. We began to collaborate, and we discovered ways to combine a focus on student interaction with academic literacy. What we created was a step-by-step procedure — with seven steps — that all teachers can use to create interactive, language-rich, and highly-engaging classrooms. The seven steps outlined in the following chapters provide examples of these important concepts.

Part 1 THE SEVEN STEPS

The Seven Steps are:

1. Teach students what to say when they don't know what to say.

2. Have students speak in complete sentences.

3. Randomize and rotate when calling on students.

4. Use total response signals.

5. Use visuals and vocabulary strategies that support your objectives.

6. Have students participate in structured conversations.

7. Have students participate in structured reading and writing activities.

+ Back to **6 & 7 with a Twist**: Include multiple perspectives.

Step 1

Teach students what to say when they don't know what to say.

As teachers who work with students from diverse backgrounds, one of the biggest challenges facing us is the phenomenon known as *learned helplessness*. It seems that as parents and teachers, we actually train students to be helpless. Every time we ask students to respond to a question or perform a task and fail to hold them accountable for their response or performance, we send them a message: you are not expected to achieve. By teaching students how to help themselves, we enable them to overcome learned helplessness and really become independent learners. It is not enough to just tell students to think for themselves and to try harder. We have to teach many of our students the language and habits of independent learners so that they can become independent learners. Teaching our students how to acquire helpful information when they are confused and teaching them to think about the steps involved in reaching a specific goal gives them skills they can use inside and outside of school. Imagine that a principal asks a group of third grade teachers to gather specific data on students from various subpopulations. The teachers look at the request and discover they don't know how to find information on the students. As a result, they write on the form, "We don't know," and put it in the principal's box. How do you think the principal would react? In the professional world, such behavior would never be acceptable.

Yet, as teachers, we have all been frustrated by calling on students who maintain a long silence as they stare at the floor, shrug their shoulders, and say, "I don't know." We are all looking for ways to banish, "I don't know," "Huh," and "What," from our classrooms. One solution that works is to teach students to respond differently when they are unsure about an answer for a question. There are specific alternatives that help students get past the "I don't know" stage. This creates an *expectation of accountable conversation.*

Here's how it works: We provide a poster for students that lists alternatives to saying "I Don't Know."

What to Say
Instead of I Don't Know

- **May I please have some more information?**
- **May I please have some time to think?**
- **Would you please repeat the question?**
- **Where could I find more information about that?**
- **May I ask a friend for help?**

On the first or second day of school, demonstrate how to use the responses and explain the procedure. Subsequently, all students are responsible for participating. After modeling the way to use the responses, explain what is meant by the *expectation of accountable conversation*. Whenever a teacher asks a question, students have two choices: either respond to the teacher or request assistance and then respond. The important principle is that students must *always respond*. They might not respond correctly and they might need some extra time or support, but opting out of the conversation is not an option.

After initially introducing the expectation of accountable conversation to students and using the poster of alternative responses in the classroom, we are ready to branch out and teach students what to say when they don't know what to say in other ways. In a science class, we might train students to ask for help and clarification during a lab. For example, "What is my job during this step?" In a language arts class, we could teach students how to ask each other questions when working in literature circles when they don't understand the conversation in the group. For example, "Could you please try to explain that in a different way?" Additionally, we could train kindergarten students to say, "Can you tell me how to_____?" when they need help in the lunch room, on the playground, or on the way to the bus. The basic idea is to give students specific sentences and questions to use in different situations so that they can independently seek help when they need it.

Is there any research that shows the effectiveness of teaching students what to say when they don't know what to say?

WHAT RESEARCH SAYS

Teaching students *what to say when they don't know what to say* is a metacognitive strategy. Research shows that the use of metacognitive strategies in the classroom has an impact on student performance. Duffy, (2002), McLaughlin, (2003), Snow, Griffin & Burns, (2005), and Vogt & Nagano, (2003) teach students to monitor their own thinking/understanding purposefully and then to choose a way to access help. Similarly, Lipson, and Wixson (2008) argue that teachers need to teach metacognitive strategies to students, model the strategy, and explain when and why the strategy should be used. Essentially, teachers first show students what to say instead of "I don't know." Then teachers show students how to use various responses. Finally, teachers demonstrate when and why students use the responses. This is particularly important to students learning English as a second language (Chamot & O'Malley, 1994; Echevarria, Vogt, & Short, 2008).

FREQUENTLY ASKED QUESTIONS

1 **How much information should I give when students ask for help?**

The goal is for students to participate as independent learners so give only the information required to accomplish that goal. We want to support students, not enable them. *Scaffolding* is support that leads to independence. *Enabling* is support that leads to dependence. Sometimes specific situations dictate when we might need to give most, or all of the information, to a student to get a response. These include: absence the day before, lack of understanding of concepts or language, or a severe learning disability.

For other learning situations, our focus is to give students the tools to answer questions without help. We might tell a student, "Look in your notes, and I'll get back to you in a minute," or "Let me give you a minute to think, and I'll get back to you." Sometimes when a student asks for help, we can simply reword or rephrase the question in simpler terms so they will be able to respond.

Take a look at the sample Teacher-Student dialogue below:

Teacher-Student Dialogue • 8th Grade

SUPPORTING STUDENTS WHO "DON'T KNOW"

Teacher: Enrique, what is the first step we might take in solving this equation?

Enrique: I don't know. *Teacher points to the poster with alternate responses.* Oh... Can I please have some more information?

Teacher: Sure, everyone look in your notes from yesterday. See if you can figure out what might be the first step we would take to solve this equation. *Teacher walks over to Enrique's desk, points to similar terms in the equation, and speaks softly to Enrique.* The first step is to group like terms. Can you repeat that for me?

Enrique: *Pointing to the similar terms.* Yeah, ...the first step is to group like terms.

Teacher: Good. Okay class, let me get your attention (*speaking in front of whole class*). Enrique, can you tell me the first step in factoring this equation?

Enrique: The first step is to group like terms.

Teacher: Thanks. Can someone show us what that looks like?

2 **How much time should I give students when they ask for time to think?**

It's easiest to have students let us know when they have had enough time. This can be accomplished by asking for a specific signal to show they are ready, like saying, "Show me a thumbs up as soon as you're ready," or "Close your book when you're ready to respond." After a student has asked for time, always be sure they are ready before calling on them. This eliminates the potential for embarrassing a student who isn't ready. If a student still needs help, we can walk over to the desk and provide one-on-one support. Another alternative is to allow students to talk to each other in a think/pair/share exercise so that the student who needs more time can get input from his peers before responding.

③ Will this strategy become a crutch for students who overuse it?

It could, if we don't remain focused on accountability and independent learning as the goal. Gradually withdrawing the support we provide when students use the strategy is key. We want to be careful, however, about being too quick to judge students' motives because they may need more assistance than we think they do. When it appears that a student is always asking for help before responding independently, we can say, "I think you can find out on your own. Look in your notes, and I'll call on you when you show me a thumbs-up."

④ What do you do with the student who absolutely refuses to respond?

It is important to pinpoint why the student is not willing to respond. Sometimes we may think a student is being noncompliant when they simply don't understand what we are asking them to do, or they didn't hear the question. Early on, some students may be embarrassed to use a new strategy for fear of looking awkward in front of their peers. When they realize that everyone will be required to use academic language in class, it becomes easier for them to participate. If a student is shy or is an English Language Learner, we can have them repeat after us or speak softly at first so that only the teacher can hear them.

The easiest way to get our noncompliant students to use alternatives to saying "I Don't Know" is to act as if they plan to participate. Just smile politely and respectfully and ask them, "Please use one of these strategies." Then wait. If they flatly refuse, model the strategy and then ask again, letting tone and body language communicate the expectation that they will participate. It's then time to look at other options: a private conference with the student, finding out if there are other issues at play, or moving ahead with another classroom management system already in place.

⑤ Won't some students always ask a friend for help and then become too dependent on others?

It depends on the student and the situation. Sometimes when working with English Language Learners or students with special needs, it can be helpful to depend on a peer for extended support while learning a new language and subject matter. If a student consistently says, "May I ask a friend for help?" and we believe they can be more independent, we say, "I think you know this. Why don't you think about it for just a minute, and I'll get back to you." If we see that support is still needed, we can walk to the desk and provide one-on-one support, or we can direct them to resources that can provide information.

⑥ What about students with special needs, do they have to respond as well?

As a general rule, we have found that all students can follow the accountability rule. If a student's individualized education plan or disability makes it impossible for them to participate, adjustments are needed. We want to be very careful here. Many times, students are capable of more than we imagine when they are given a chance.

7 Will these strategies slow down my instruction as I provide assistance for struggling learners?

When we start to apply the expectation of accountable conversation, it does slow down instruction, especially when students are just getting used to the procedure. Students often struggle as they try to master thinking independently and as they become responsible for learning. This is especially true for upper elementary and secondary students. Many of our students have never been expected to participate in class discussions. Expect it to take some time for students to adjust and feel safe responding.

We all feel the pressure of the current climate of accountability. In this environment, it is stressful to have to slow down the pace of instruction every time a student doesn't know the answer to a question. It might seem like a good idea to rush through the curriculum to make sure we "cover" everything needed for the assessment test. The problem, as Wiggins and McTighe (2005) would tell us, is that when we do this, we don't think enough about "uncovering" the subject, and the curriculum suffers.

Even when we carefully monitor our pacing and thoughtfully plan the curriculum, we may struggle with effective ways to handle a student's requests for more information. One strategy that benefits students, keeps the pace of the lesson, and still provides support is "Turn and Tell Five." Here's how it works: When we call on a student and the student requests more information, we tell the whole class to turn to the person next to them and discuss possible answers. Students are given five seconds to speak to one another. We then call on the same student who requested information and give them an opportunity to respond.

Here's an example of how it might sound in a typical classroom:

Teacher-Student Dialogue • First Grade

TURN AND TELL FIVE

Teacher: Yesterday, we were learning about communities. Can anyone remember an example of a community? Let's see ...*Teacher draws Billy's name out of a stack of cards* Billy?

Billy: I forgot.

Teacher: Can you use the strategy we talked about earlier? Remember the poster?

Billy: Oh yeah. Can I please have some more information?

Teacher: Sure Billy. Everyone turn to your partners and give an example of a community; you have five seconds. I'm going to count down with my fingers. Ready, go. *Teacher uses his/her fingers to count from five to one, then speaks to Billy directly.* Billy, are you ready?

Billy: Yeah.

Teacher: Okay, everybody, eyes on me. Billy, can you give me an example of a community?

Billy: Yeah, families are communities, right?

Teacher: Yes, great example! Let's see who will be picked to give me another example...

Step 2

Have students **speak in complete sentences.**

This simple expectation dramatically improves the quality of interactions in our classroom. When we encourage our students to use complete sentences, they think in complete thoughts. They link new words to new concepts and are able to practice using academic language structures.

Picture, for a moment, a student named Natalie. She is an eighth grader in a U.S. History class. The teacher calls on Natalie and asks her to explain what the class just read. Natalie thinks for a moment and then says,

Ok now, there were the British ones... and the other ones ... and they didn't like each other, with the taxation representation thingy...and they were all throwing tea into the water and were mad and stuff and wanted you know...independence and everything. They called it a tea party, but they didn't have no balloons or nothing.

Any eighth grade teacher knows that this kind of response is all too common. Predictably, when Natalie writes her thoughts on paper, she will write exactly the same way. She simply does not know how to communicate using formal academic language. It's very hard for students to write in a way they cannot speak. By providing students with opportunities to communicate, we give them the gift of academic language and a passport to communicate in the professional world. The beginning of the process is learning to communicate our thoughts completely by using complete sentences.

Every single interaction in the classroom between the teacher and the students, and among students, does not require complete sentences. Sometimes, informal language is appropriate, even in professional settings. However, students must be given experience in using formal language. It is very important to provide ample opportunities in class that require students to use complete sentences in oral communication. In doing so, students learn how to develop their thoughts and use formal language structures.

Here's how it might sound in a typical classroom:

Teacher-Student Dialogue • Fifth Grade

COMPLETE SENTENCES

Teacher: We've been looking at fractions, and we have been talking about how to add fractions. What was the first step in adding fractions? *Teacher draws Erminda's name from a stack.* Erminda?

Erminda: The first step in adding fractions is to find a common denominator.

Teacher: Exactly. When we look at these two fractions, one fourth and one third, what would the common denominator be?....*Teacher draws Lashaunda's name from a stack.* Lashaunda?

Lashaunda: 12. *(continued next page)*

Teacher: *Smiling and using a supportive tone.* Could I have that in a sentence please?

Lashaunda: The common denominator of three and four is twelve.

Teacher: Thanks, Lashaunda. How did Lashaunda find the common denominator? *Teacher draws Aaron's name from a stack.* Aaron? How do you think Lashaunda found the common denominator?

Aaron: ...with three and four. *Teacher waits a moment and Aaron rephrases his answer.* I mean, Lashaunda found the common denominator by multiplying three and four.

One way to support students as they learn to respond with complete sentences is to provide them with a sentence stem. A sentence stem is a short phrase that gives students the beginning of a sentence and helps them structure a response.

Using sentence stems dramatically changes the quality and tone of a classroom because it helps students become increasingly more comfortable using academic language for expression.

Here are examples of sentence stems:

Question	Stem
Why does inertia have a particularly large effect in this situation?	Inertia has a large effect in this situation because ...
How would you approach solving this equation?	My approach to solving this equation would be to ...
What is your opinion?	My opinion is ...
How would you justify your answer?	I would justify my answer by ...

Is there any research that shows how using complete sentences when speaking and writing has an effect on student achievement?

WHAT RESEARCH SAYS

Research indicates that in order for students to use content language accurately in their speaking and writing, they must hear the language multiple times and in multiple contexts (NICHD, 2000). Having students speak in complete sentences provides a means for students to hear content-area vocabulary used in context, not only by the teacher, but also by their peers.

The National Literacy Panel on Language Minority Children and Youth (2006) highlighted the significant relationship between oral proficiency in English and reading and writing proficiency. When students are proficient in oral language, they are more proficient in their reading and writing (Geva, 2006). The research-based SIOP Model (Echevarria, Vogt, & Short, 2008) demonstrates that students need frequent opportunities for interaction in order to encourage elaborated responses to lesson concepts. A classroom culture that requires the use of complete sentences routinely fosters student elaboration while a classroom using one-word responses to questions does not.

FREQUENTLY ASKED QUESTIONS

1 **Will it strain classroom conversation and limit students' ability to express themselves if we expect them to rephrase answers using complete sentences?**

No. Rather than limiting classroom conversation, the expectation of using complete sentences in the classroom actually enhances the free flow of ideas. Elaboration is rare in classrooms where one-word and short phrase answers are the norm. In this situation, students do not hear other students regularly communicating with complete thoughts and sentences. Instead, they hear phrases and fragments in response to teacher questions. In contrast, when complete thoughts are the norm, students quickly become more comfortable elaborating and expressing their ideas. When students are asked open-ended questions at a higher level, they are able to say much more by using complete sentences.

We do need to be careful, however, not to overdo the use of complete sentences in class. We do want students to respond in complete sentences when we ask them questions directly during whole-class interactions, but we do not expect them to communicate with complete sentences in every interaction. A simple guideline is to make sure that every time a new question or topic is introduced in a discussion, it is good to reiterate the expectation for using complete sentences. If we are having an open discussion, we can relax and allow the free flow of ideas.

Here's how it might sound in a typical classroom:

Teacher-Student Dialogue • 12th Grade Government

BALANCING THE USE OF COMPLETE SENTENCES

Teacher: We've been talking about the tension between federal and state governments in the American system. What was one source of those problems? *Teacher draws Ryan's name out of a stack.* Ryan?

Ryan: The Constitution. *Teacher pauses and glances at a poster that says,* "Please express your thoughts in complete sentences." One source of the tension was the Constitution. Didn't it give powers to both groups?

Teacher: What do you mean?

Ryan: Both have some power, like the federal government can do some things and state governments can do other things.

Teacher: What kinds of things can the federal government do? *Linda raises her hand.*

Linda: Control the foreign policy.

Teacher: Can you tell me more about that?

FAQS

2 **Do students with disabilities, English Language Learners, and students with interrupted formal education (SIFE) have to express themselves using complete sentences too?**

Yes! Unless a student has a disability with an Individualized Education Plan (IEP) that indicates otherwise, expect all students to participate. With a few simple techniques, everyone can be included in this process. Students learning a new language have to negotiate content and language structures simultaneously. When they are in a classroom with native speakers, they need to be provided with more support. Giving sentence starters like, "The answer is..." and "I think..." improves communication abilities for English Language Learners. This technique eliminates juggling unfamiliar language structures, and it makes communication easier for students. Another strategy is to allow students to whisper answers that are repeated to the whole class. They feel safe, supported, and involved.

3 **What if students refuse to respond with the expectation of using complete sentences?**

If students are given an adequate rationale, most of them will come on board. Students need a reason to practice speaking in complete sentences in the classroom, and the reason has to make sense to them. One helpful method is to talk to students about the importance of sounding professional in order to achieve success in life. To underscore the importance of complete sentences, we offer two examples of a job interview. After reading the interviews, students decide which applicant they think will get the job, and they tell why. Discussing this scenario with students usually helps to create buy-in for the strategy. If students are still resistant to participation, talk to them individually to explain sensible reasons for using the technique.

Applicant A

Employer: So, tell me about your work experience.

Applicant: Burger King.

Employer: What did you do at Burger King?

Applicant: The register, the grill, and the drive-through.

Employer: Did you enjoy working there?

Applicant: Yeah.

Applicant B

Employer: So, tell me about your work experience.

Applicant: My work experience includes working at Burger King.

Employer: What did you do at Burger King?

Applicant: While I was at Burger King I worked at the register; I cooked on the grill; and I also was able to work in the drive-through sometimes.

Employer: Did you enjoy working there?

Applicant: Yes, I enjoyed it very much.

4 **When should I introduce this strategy to my students?**

It's always best to introduce the practice of using complete sentences at the beginning of the school year. Explain the *expectation of accountable conversation* with students first and then explain how they are expected to participate in class discussions. Many teachers have found implementation easier than they thought once the goal and the expectations of the strategy were clearly communicated to students.

"*We should not convert America to an ethanol-based economy because...*"

Step 3

Randomize and rotate when calling on students.

Many teachers have struggled with finding ways to manage a classroom full of diverse learners. The same few students always raise their hands to respond as the rest of the class sits. We often end up calling on the energetic participators because they usually know the answer, and it allows us to maintain the pace of our lesson. Every so often we insist that other students respond, and we are met with frustration, anxiety, or a blank stare.

Solution 1: Randomizing

Randomizing is one effective way to overcome this problem. It requires very little planning. We create a simple system, like using index cards or Popsicle™ sticks with each student's name, and rely on that system when we call on students. This changes the way we ask questions. We avoid using phrases like:

"Who can tell me…?"

"Let's see who knows…."

"Does anyone know …"

"Can someone tell the class…"

For the most part, these phrases encourage the participatory students who continue to shout out and dominate discussion. Our goal is to have everyone involved in discussions so that we can assess all students' understanding of concepts, not just those students who enjoy participating. When we do not use random selection to assess students, we are only checking the understanding of a few highly motivated students. When randomizing, the questioning technique then looks like this:

1. Ask the question.
2. Pause.
3. Select a student to respond using a random selection system.

It's important to ask questions without solicitation of volunteers. In some cases, it actually helps to explicitly ask students **not** to raise hands; this eliminates the temptation to call only on those who volunteer. Pausing after the question gives everyone a chance to think, and it creates some **positive tension** as students wonder who will be chosen. Next, we use random selection, by drawing an index card from a pile, for example. This ensures that all students are paying attention and have a fair chance to be called on to respond. Asking questions in this way promotes higher student engagement and more accurate assessment of student understanding. With this method, students grow accustomed to always being prepared to respond, and we grow accustomed to using cards or sticks whenever we ask questions or have discussions.

Solution 2: Rotating

Using a rotation strategy works best with some classroom discussions. Spencer Kagan's *Numbered Heads Together* is an easy way to get everyone involved and avoid the problems of calling on the same students again and again.

Here are the steps.

1. Divide students into groups of four.
2. Ask students to count off within the group (1-4) so each person has a number.
3. Ask a question.
4. Give groups a chance to talk to each other about the answer.
5. Ask one number to stand up in each group. For example, "All Ones, please stand."
6. Have the number One person report for the group.
7. Instruct students to respond with this sentence stem if they have the same response as another group: "We agree that _____ because…

Repeat the procedure with other questions until each number from 1-4 has been called, giving every person an opportunity to speak for their group. Numbered heads together is used best with open-ended questions that have more than one possible response. Of course, all students should share their answers in complete sentences.

Some other ways to randomize and rotate include: marking a seating chart as students are called on, numbering desks, and using computer programs to randomly select student names. The important thing is not which system we use, but that we have a system in place. It is important to include everyone. Without a system, total participation is impossible.

There are times when it may be helpful to have an open dialogue without using index cards or seating charts. Similarly, teachers may like the energy of students calling out answers and freely exchanging ideas. These discussions can be positive experiences for students, but rarely for all students. If we do not have a system in place, there are students being left out. Those students are usually the at-risk pupils, students with special needs, and English Language Learners, all of whom would most benefit from active participation.

Is there any research that connects the use of randomization techniques to student achievement?

WHAT RESEARCH SAYS

Student engagement is highly correlated to student achievement. Schmoker (2006) and Bickel and Bickel (1986) state that learning increases when students are focused on tasks during instruction. Rotating responses is particularly helpful in maintaining accountability during cooperative tasks (Johnson & Johnson, 1999). In a study conducted by McDougal and Cordeiro (1993), students who attended lectures that utilized random questioning out-performed similar students in classes where random oral questioning was not used by 20%. The researchers suggest that random oral questioning increases student preparedness, attentiveness, and achievement (McDougal and Cordeiro, 1993).

Step

FREQUENTLY ASKED QUESTIONS

1 How often should we use randomizing and rotating for questioning?

In order to check for student understanding, randomizing and rotating should take place in every classroom whenever there is whole-class discussion. Other kinds of questioning are effective for motivating students, getting new ideas on the table, creating resources, and generating creative energy. But, if we want to check for understanding, we must randomize, or rotate, whom we select to respond to questions.

It's not necessary to randomize every single question asked. A helpful guideline is to call on students randomly every time a new question or a new topic is introduced. If students want to add thoughts or responses to an existing topic, it's all right for them to volunteer ideas. If we want to generate a flow of ideas on a topic after using random selection, we can open the class discussion to all.

2 What should we do about students who blurt out answers?

Teaching students to refrain from blurting out answers is a skill that students can learn just like everything else they learn in school. A good starting point is to explain why we want students to avoid calling out answers. Setting up a role-play with two students having a conversation and a third student who constantly interrupts provides a clear example for students. After watching this role-play, ask students what they think of the interruptions and have them write their responses. As you review the responses, most students will describe such behavior as rude, unkind, anti-social, immature, etc. Explain that when we call on a student by name, we have begun a conversation. If others choose to talk over the conversation, they are interrupting, and this behavior shows them in an unfavorable light.

With secondary students, it is unrealistic to tell students they can never talk without raising their hands. This is not the way academic discourse usually takes place among adults in professional and university settings. There are some types of discussions where raising hands or waiting for the speaker to call on someone inhibits the free flow of ideas. In order to maintain a respectful classroom culture, we want students to avoid calling out and interrupting others on these three occasions:

1. when we are using a randomzing system
2. when we call on another student by name
3. when another student has not finished expressing ideas

Most students see these guidelines as reasonable and agree that they build a safer classroom environment for students to answer questions and express views. Establishing these guidelines early in the year and enforcing them consistently is critical to their success.

Part 1 | Step 3

FAQS

3 Should we place the index cards and Popsicle™ sticks back in the stack or should we take them out one-by-one to make sure everyone gets a chance to respond?

Different teachers have different answers to this question. Some students know they will no longer be called upon when their stick or card is removed, and they check out of the discussion. This problem can be solved if you:

1. Return the cards to the bottom of the stack. Draw mostly from the top half of the stack, occasionally drawing from the bottom so that student names have the potential of occurring again.

2. Use a "double bucket" for the sticks. Let the outside bucket hold the student names who have not yet been called, and let the inside bucket hold student names who have already been called. Draw from the outside bucket during discussions; occasionally draw from the inside bucket so that names can be called again.

3. Combine randomizing and rotating. During a discussion using numbered heads together, call on all the Twos to share. Afterward, randomly call on a student to respond to what the Two said by using the sentence starters: "I agree with _____ that …" or "I disagree with _____ that…"

4 What about students who are way behind their peers? Won't it embarrass them if we call on them?

Teaching students what to say when they don't know the answer (Step 1, p. 9) solves this problem. Students can feel confident when called upon because even if they do not have the answer, they always have an appropriate response, such as, "May I please have some more information?"

5 Will it discourage students who want to share if I randomize and rotate responses? Will they not want to participate if I redirect them when they blurt out answers?

Students who like to talk and share in class are sometimes frustrated at the beginning when they can no longer be the center of the teacher's attention. Many students are used to dominating classroom discussions, and their sense of self-worth is tied to their ability to answer questions and share thoughts. Sometimes these students will complain about the use of randomization techniques. When we vary our questioning techniques, include Numbered Heads Together, and increase the amount of student-to-student interaction, these students will have their needs met.

Students learning to listen actively to one another is an additional benefit of randomizing and rotating student responses. Sometimes students who dominate discussions don't realize that other students who are more quiet or less verbal have great ideas to share. By giving them a chance to slow down and hear what other students have to say, they learn both patience and tolerance for another student's point-of-view. The students who don't often share in discussions learn that their views are valuable and that they can successfully contribute to a healthy exchange of ideas. These skills are essential if we hope to build argumentative literacy for our students.

*"Will the number Threes
from each team
please stand?"*

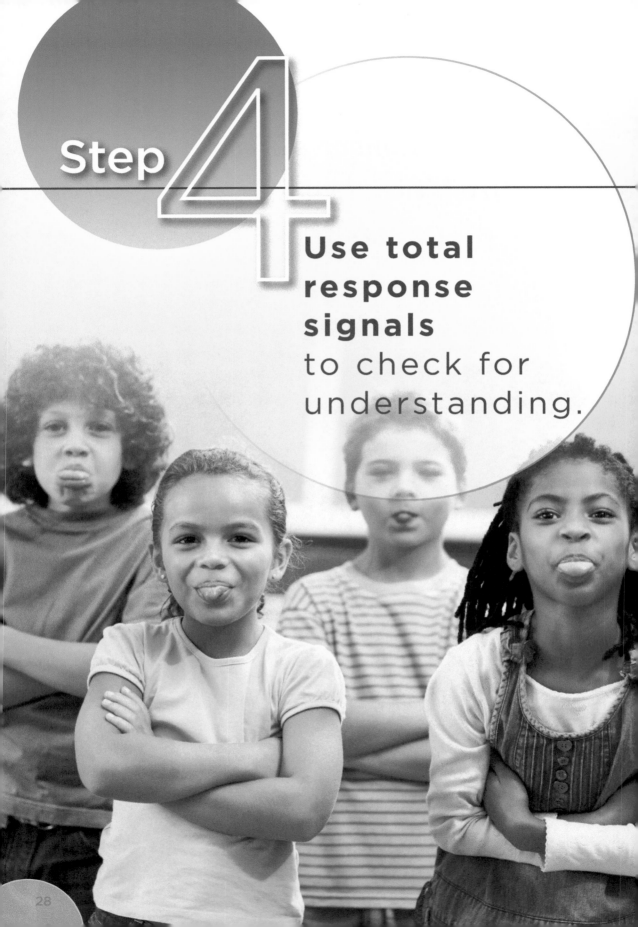

Step **4**

Use total response signals to check for understanding.

Total response signals are cues students can use to indicate they are ready to respond to a question or ready to move on to new material. Response signals allow students to prepare for oral or written participation in a non-threatening way, and they provide a very effective tool for gauging student understanding in real time.

There are three elements of an effective total response signal.

Total: Total response signals include every student in the classroom: at risk pupils, ELLs, students with special needs, gifted students, oppositionally defiant students, and students with interrupted formal education. Total means everyone.

Response: Every student will make a choice. After questions are posed, students are given an opportunity to make a decision. Students think through what they know to make choices.

Signal: Once students have responded or made decisions, they will give a response with a visual signal. The signal must be clear enough so that we can immediately survey how many students can respond to the question or decision.

Here's how it might sound in a typical classroom:

Teacher-Student Dialogue • Second Grade
TOTAL RESPONSE SIGNALS

Teacher: Okay, everyone, take a look at the map of our school on your desks. Show me thumbs-up as soon as you can find the principal's office. *Students begin to put their thumbs up as they find the principal's office. The teacher notices a few students struggling, walks to their desks, and points out the location of the principal's office with her finger. These students put their thumbs up.* Okay, I see everyone has found the principal's office. Now, I'm going to give you a sentence starter. I'm going to select someone to finish this sentence; the principal's office is next to... *Teacher selects Popsicle™ stick from bucket.* Felicia?

Felicia: The principal's office is next to the water fountain.

Teacher: Thanks, Felicia. Now, everyone find the compass on your school map. It looks like this picture on the board. Show me a thumbs-up when you can find it ...

Total response signals enable us to consistently check for student understanding. We think of them as instant ongoing assessments used throughout a lesson. With response signals, we don't have to wait for the quiz, test, worksheet, or writing assignment to find out how well our students understand a topic. We can immediately check for understanding and see who is ready to move on and who still needs help. There are four basic types of response signals:

Written Response: Students write their responses on paper, sticky notes, cards, white boards, or chalk boards and hold them up so they are visible to the teacher.

Ready Response: Students show they have finished a task or are ready to begin a new task. For example, the Thinker's Chin means that students keep their hands on their chins until they finish thinking and are ready to respond to a question. When the hand is removed from the chin, they are ready.

Making Choices: Students show their response to a specific set of choices using a physical object or signal. For example, give students letter cards, labeled A, B, C, and D when reviewing a multiple-choice test. After reading a question, ask students to show their choice. We can instantly see how students respond to each question.

Ranking: Students show their relative agreement and disagreement with particular statements. For example, ask students if they agree or disagree with the following statement, "We should make a table before setting up an equation to solve this problem." Have students hold up a five to signal agreement and a one to signal disagreement. Ask students who are undecided to hold up a two, three, or four. Ask students to be ready to explain their reasoning.

The chart below gives specific examples of each type of response signal.

Written Response	• Hold up Paper
	• White Boards
	• Personal Chalk Boards
	• Answers on Cards
Ready Response	• Hands Up When Ready
	• Hands Down When Ready
	• Thinker's Chin (hand off chin when ready)
	• Stand When You Are Ready
	• Sit When You Are Ready
	• Put your Pen on your Paper When Ready
	• Put your Pen Down When You Are Finished
	• All Eyes on Teacher
	• Heads Down
Making Choices	• Open Hand/Closed Hand
	• Thumbs Up/Thumbs Down
	• Pens Up/Pens Down
	• Number Wheels
	• Green Card/Red Card
	• Move to the Corner/Spot You Agree/Disagree with
	• Letter or Number Card Choices on a Metal Ring – A, B, C, D or 1, 2, 3, 4
Ranking	• Rank with Your Fingers
	• Rank with Your Arm (the higher, the better)
	• Line Up According to Response
	• Knocking/Clapping/Cheering

Is there any research that shows the effect of response signals on student achievement?

WHAT RESEARCH SAYS

Research demonstrates that student engagement increases attention which increases student achievement (Jensen, 2005). Active response signals are a powerful way to get students' attention because they connect physical movement with mental processes. Response signals have also been shown to have a highly significant effect on achievement for inner-city students during whole class science instruction (Gardner, Heward & Grossi, 1996), and on special needs students during whole class math instruction (Christle & Schuster, 2003). In addition, research emphasizes the beneficial effect of "clickers," a computer-based system of total response signals, on student achievement (Caldwell, 1994).

FREQUENTLY ASKED QUESTIONS

① How do you make sure students use response signals correctly? Won't many of them show a signal even though they're not ready just because all the other students are showing a signal?

This can be a problem if we aren't intentional about how to use total response signals. It is crucial to structure the use of response signals so that students are relaxed and honest when they use them. We also have to be respectful and encouraging when students do not show us a signal. If we ask students to raise their hands when they are ready to respond and many students are still sitting with their hands down, we have to be supportive and assume they would raise their hands if they had a response. At this point, we can rephrase the question, or ask everyone to put their hands down, clarify the information, and then ask the question again.

Providing variety for students to respond after a response signal helps students participate authentically. Sometimes students can share their thoughts with each other; other times we randomly select a student to share with the class. If we always have students share with each other after giving us a response signal, many will show signals even though they are not ready to respond; they know they can rely on their partners for ideas. Randomizing after a response signal reduces this tendency.

This is how the situation might sound in a typical classroom:

Teacher-Student Dialogue • Sixth Grade Language Arts

HOLDING STUDENTS ACCOUNTABLE FOR USE OF TOTAL RESPONSE SIGNALS

Teacher: Okay, what do you think Stanley's motive was for leaving home? Raise your hand as soon as you have thought about a reason for Stanley to leave. *All students raise their hands. Teacher randomly selects Bryce's name from stack of cards.* Bryce, what do you think?

Bryce: May I please have some more information?

Teacher: I think maybe the directions I gave weren't clear. Let me try again. Okay class, raise your hand as soon as you have an answer. Please don't raise your hand until you are ready to respond. That way I can make sure everybody's ready before I make a choice. *Most students raise their hands. Some are still not raised.*

Teacher: Okay, let's talk again about motive. Motive is the reason you do something. Think about what we read yesterday. Remember when Stanley left home? Why do you think he left? Raise your hand when you can finish this sentence: Stanley's motive for leaving was... *All students raise their hands.* Bryce, what do you think?

Bryce: Stanley's motive for leaving was that he thought everyone was mad at him.

2 **What if students still won't show a response signal, even after ample time is given?**

If students won't show a response signal after ample time is given, we ask everyone to put their hands down or stop showing a signal. Then we repeat the concept, the question, or the instructions. Next, we ask if anyone needs help understanding, and we give students a chance to clarify misunderstandings with someone sitting near them. We then give the response signal again. If there are still a few students who don't understand, we might work with them individually or ask if they understand what they are being instructed to do. Sometimes it is possible to think decisions and tasks are easier than they are for our students. If more than two students delay too long in showing a response signal, we need to think about how well students really understand the task or the concept. The whole purpose of a response signal is to assess student understanding. If students are telling us they don't understand, then the signals are working well. The lack of response signals tells us where we need to re-teach and refocus our instruction.

3 **Won't students just look to see what other students' signals or answers are and then copy those responses?**

Yes, many students will do that. However, there are some strategies that can be used to overcome this problem. One strategy to eliminate mimicking when using letter cards is to print the letters on one side only; another is to have students sit in rows or at tables in positions where they cannot easily see how other students are responding. An alternative is to ask students to show their choices on a count of three or when we say, "Go." When students realize the signals are used to help support them when they don't understand and to find out what they think about various ideas, it is more likely they will show their understanding and choices with the signals.

4 **What about students with special needs who can't use certain signals?**

We need to be sensitive to what our students are physically capable of doing, and we have to avoid putting students in awkward situations by choosing to use total response signals. If a student has limited mobility and the response signal involves moving around the room, we want to make sure to give that student other options to express choice. If a student's level of cognitive development limits understanding or choices, modify or clarify the question in such a way that special needs students can participate in the conversation meaningfully.

Step 5

Use visuals and vocabulary strategies that support your objectives.

Teachers everywhere fill their "bag of tricks" with as many strategies and tools as possible in order to help their students learn new material efficiently. Step Five is comprised of tools that make a huge impact on all students, especially struggling learners. Let's look at using visuals and vocabulary strategies and how they help us meet our teaching objectives effectively.

Use Visuals

Incorporating visuals in our lessons dramatically increases student ability to understand class lessons and discussions. It has been said that "a picture is worth a thousand words," and often this is true. Photos, maps, drawings, movie clips, and concrete objects give students access to content in spite of possible barriers such as lack of background on the subject or limited English proficiency. If the content objective, for example, is to explain safe lab procedures, showing photos of "safe" and "unsafe" activities will give students a stronger grasp of the content.

Another really effective visual tool is the graphic organizer. Graphic organizers provide a way for students to organize facts, ideas, and concepts that help them make sense of the content. You probably make use of some of these already. Graphic organizers can be used before instruction

to provide a scaffold for new material, and they can show how much students already know about a topic. During instruction, they can be used to help students organize key information. After instruction, graphic organizers help students connect prior knowledge with new information and determine relationships between the two.

There are many types of graphic organizers that are available in books and on the Internet. Some of these include: story maps, Venn diagrams, spider maps, T-charts, and KWL charts. When introducing a new type of graphic organizer, be sure to model its use and provide time for guided practice. As students become more skilled at using the organizers, they can create their own variations.

One strategy that promotes the use of visuals and takes very little advance planning is Point and Talk. This strategy helps clarify meaning for new concepts. Simply draw or show a visual of the key concept for each lesson. Keep it posted throughout the unit of study and consistently point back to it. Let's use a Language Arts concept to illustrate this strategy. When teaching plot development, use a mountain like the one below as a visual, and point to each stage as it is discussed. This gives students a visual anchor that will help simplify this vocabulary-dense concept.

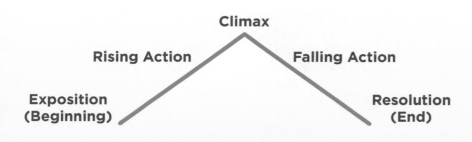

Climax

Rising Action Falling Action

Exposition
(Beginning)

Resolution
(End)

Develop Vocabulary

In the introduction, we discussed the importance of incorporating academic vocabulary in all of our lessons. A good rule of thumb is to introduce and display at least two new words per lesson. Here are two specific strategies that build academic vocabulary:

Scanning

Scanning is a powerful, quick, and efficient tool used to build academic language skills for students. This strategy teaches students essential words for understanding new content minutes before they encounter the words in a text. With this strategy, student achievement is increased by 33% as compared to students who did not use the strategy. Here's how it works:

1. The students survey a text from back to front looking for unfamiliar words.

2. The teacher generates a list of three to ten unfamiliar terms based on the students' survey.

3. The teacher writes short student-friendly definitions for the terms, giving definitions that match the way the word is used in the context of the passage.

4. The students practice pronouncing the words during a choral reading with the teacher.

5. The students read the passage.

6. The students use some of the words during the speaking and writing tasks in the lesson. For example, students might include scan words as they discuss the text with a partner, or they can use them in a written summary of the text.

Here's an example of how it might sound in a typical classroom:

Teacher-Student Dialogue • Eighth Grade Math

SCANNING

Teacher: *Provides students with handout containing word problems after modeling examples for the class.* Okay everyone, look at the handout, and let's do a quick scan of unfamiliar terms. Start at the bottom, scan toward the top, and circle two or more terms that you or someone else in class cannot define. *Students begin circling words on their handout.* Okay, I can see most of you have found a few words. Enrique, tell me one of the words you selected.

Enrique: Vehicle. *Teacher pauses and glances at poster saying, "Please express your thoughts in complete sentences."* I selected the word *vehicle.*

Teacher: *Writes down vehicle on dry erase board.* Thanks. Erica, what was one of the words you selected?

Erica: I selected the word *expression.*

Teacher: *Writes down the word expression on dry erase board.* Okay, does anyone else have a word that we should include? Brian?

Brian: I'm not sure what a *coordinate* plane is. I know we talked about it. Is that just like the graph we make of different problems?

Teacher: Kind of. Let's write that down too. *Writes coordinate plane.* Anyone else? Okay. Can anyone think of a short definition for the word *vehicle*? Just call out an answer.

Students: *A few students speak out loud.* A car, a truck. Something that moves you around.

Teacher: Let's write, "something that carries you around, like a car or truck." *Writes definition.* Okay, what does *expression* mean?

Students: *Calling out.* Equation, number sentence.

Teacher: Okay. Let's write, "a number sentence." That's what we usually have been calling expressions. *Writes definition.* Can someone raise a hand and tell me what a coordinate plane is?

Ted: Isn't a *coordinate plane* the plane that has all the x and y coordinates on it?

Teacher: Basically. Let's write something like, "the flat space with all the x and y coordinates."

Teacher: *At the end of the class period...* Okay, go ahead and fill out your math journals. Your sentence starter is on the board. Make sure you include at least one word from our scan: *vehicle, expression, or coordinate plane.*

When students read new written material, they often find unfamiliar vocabulary. To eliminate stumbling over new words, we use scanning before a reading exercise begins. It doesn't take very much time for students to get used to this procedure, and it quickly builds student understanding of academic vocabulary. Scanning gives students some control over the vocabulary we emphasize, and it gives us the chance to focus on learning what students don't know instead of re-emphasizing what they already do know.

Marzano's Six-Step Process

In *Building Academic Vocabulary* (Marzano, 2004), Marzano outlines a comprehensive approach to learning the content-specific academic vocabulary, or the brick words that students encounter in their reading. The first three steps help us introduce new terms during the first lesson; the last three steps help students practice and reinforce those terms over time. These steps are easily remembered as the terms: *Describe, Describe, Draw, Do, Discuss, Play.*

Step 1 – Describe: Instead of giving a formal definition of a vocabulary word or term, teachers give students a description or explanation of the word or term using examples and visuals. The goal is to appeal to learners of all types in order to help them understand new vocabulary.

Step 2 - Describe: Ask students to give a description or explanation of a vocabulary word or term using their own words. By listening/reading student descriptions/explanations, we can assess mastery, or we can provide help to make the words comprehensible. Students record descriptions in their personal notebooks to reference later.

Step 3 - Draw: Ask students to draw a representation of the new vocabulary word or term. Acceptable ways to complete this task include: drawing pictures, designing symbols, making graphics, creating cartoons, finding a visual on the Internet or in a magazine. These tasks can be done individually or in groups.

Step 4 - Do: To give students more practice using new vocabulary words or terms, have them participate in activities such as: identifying prefixes, suffixes, synonyms, antonyms, related words, and additional visuals.

Step 5 - Discuss: Have students discuss the vocabulary words or terms as they work with/in partners, triads, or groups. This type of vocabulary discussion is more effective when it is structured. Additionally, monitoring student discussions clears up any confusion students may have about the words or terms.

Step 6 – Play: Students participate in games that reinforce deep understanding of the new vocabulary words or terms. Examples of games include: Jeopardy, Wordo (like bingo), Charades, Pictionary, Scrabble, etc.

Scanning and Marzano's Six-Step Process are two ways to teach vocabulary, but there are many other effective strategies. It doesn't matter which strategies we use as long as we remain focused on our goal: helping students develop a deep understanding of academic vocabulary so they can achieve in school and communicate in the real world.

Another strategy that supports teaching objectives

is using sentence stems. This strategy helps students form complete sentences, and it allows students to grow accustomed to the kind of words and phrases usually found in academic English. Most importantly, however, sentence stems give students an opportunity to practice using new vocabulary words and terms in *context*. For example, when learning about the states of matter, this sentence stem, "One property of a solid is…" gives students the chance to practice using the words *property* and *solid* in the correct context. The process of using a sentence stem begins when the teacher provides it as a starting point for a response. Students can use sentence stems for oral and written responses. At first, students will only use sentence stems when required to do so, but over time they quickly become a part of classroom routines.

There are two types of sentence stems, general and specific. A general stem can be used in any content area. We use general stems to find out what our students are thinking and also to determine the amount of background knowledge a student has on any given topic. Examples of general stems are: "I learned….," "I already know…," and "I agree/disagree with _____ because…" Unlike general stems, specific sentence stems are tied to a particular content area or lesson. We use specific stems to check for understanding of the learning objectives. Examples of specific stems are: "One cause of the Civil War was…," "Photosynthesis is…," "I think _____ is the protagonist because…" Using both general and specific sentence stems gives students many risk-free opportunities to speak and to write using academic language.

General Stem	Specific Stem
I learned …	I learned a new way to factor …
I already know …	I already know that authors use characterization to …
I agree/disagree with ___ because …	I agree/disagree with Dora the Explorer's decision to choose the iceberg because …

We have also found it helpful to look at our assessments as a guide to developing sentence stems for students to use. Both standardized assessments and local assessments often have sentence structures and terminology that are unfamiliar to students. We can look at some of the assessment questions and then create sentence stems to give students a chance to practice using academic language.

Examples include:

Test Question	Sentence Stem
Which word from paragraph 2 means the same thing as sinister?	The word from the paragraph that means the same thing as sinister is ...
What speed record did Alma exceed by exactly 4.66 miles per hour?	The record Alma exceeded by exactly 4.66 miles per hour was ...
How did the invention of the printing press affect the flow of ideas in Europe in the 1500s?	The invention of the printing press affected the flow of ideas in Europe in the 1500's by ...

Sentence stems provide a framework for students to gradually use increasing amounts of academic language. When our students have opportunities to practice using the words and phrases they will encounter on an assessment, they are better prepared for those assessments because the language used is familiar to them.

By strategically using general and specific sentence stems, we change the way students talk. When we change the way they talk, we open the door to new ways of thinking.

Is there any research that connects the use of vocabulary strategies and sentence stems to student achievement?

WHAT RESEARCH SAYS

Graphic organizers are highly effective when used appropriately.

Fountas and Pinnell (2001) state that when content is illustrated with diagrams, the information will be better maintained over a period of time. Meyen, Vergason, and Whelan (1996) report that graphic organizers serve as an organized display that makes information easier to understand and to learn.

Students with learning disabilities often have difficulty recalling newly-learned content and with making connections between details and broad concepts. In addition, they often find that math facts and procedures can be very frustrating to learn and remember. Gagnon and Maccini (2000) found that using graphic organizers in math class may lessen students' difficulties with math concepts.

Pre-teaching terms enhances student reading comprehension. Stahl and Fairbanks (1986), demonstrate that student comprehension soars 33% when specific key terms are introduced prior to reading and learning (as cited in Marzano, Pickering & Pollock, 2001, *Classroom Instruction That Works*). Therefore, pre-teaching terms is important.

Using vocabulary strategies and sentence stems improve student achievement for English Language Learners, who often find academic concepts especially difficult (Echevarria, Vogt, & Short, 2008).

Step 5 FREQUENTLY ASKED QUESTIONS

1 Some of the content I teach is very abstract and does not have a clear visual representation to go with it. What should I do?

A great place to generate ideas for visuals that support abstract concepts is the Internet. Typing key words from your content into Google Images, for example, will produce many pictures, photos, and graphic representations. Your colleagues and school librarian are also excellent resources. Asking students to create a visual for the content being taught can also produce fantastic images for use in subsequent years.

2 Should we have students look up the words that have been scanned from a dictionary and have them define the words on their own?

No. This will take too much time. Scanning is a quick process. Our goal is to give students the meaning of the scan words within the context of what they are reading for that specific lesson. Having students look up isolated words in the dictionary does not meet this goal because they will encounter multiple definitions riddled with more unfamiliar words.

3 Why does the scan process seem backwards, going from the end to the beginning of a passage?

Beginning the scan process from back to front helps the student focus on unfamiliar words and terms without reading the content. The unfamiliar words and terms will be more identifiable using the back to front process because it makes the scan procedure move along quickly.

4 The vocabulary techniques (scanning and Six-Step Process) are a nice idea, but will they take too much time?

They do take time, but the time spent using these techniques is well worth the investment because student comprehension and understanding are increased. When students scan for unfamiliar words before reading a text, they will be confident and successful during the reading task. When working with content-specific vocabulary in multiple ways, students gain a deeper understanding of the words, and they internalize their meanings.

5 Shouldn't we do something more with vocabulary words so that students will really learn them?

Yes, we can put them on an interactive word wall posted in the classroom. A word wall is a place for lists of words that changes over time. On the word wall, we can list scan words from written material, key content concepts, or words that might be helpful for students to use in writing or in conversation. Some of us put short definitions next to the words, others don't. The most important thing about word wall words is to be sure that students have multiple opportunities to use the words when they write and speak.

1. Offer class/individual incentives or praise for using the words/terms.
2. Require the use of specific words/terms in a warm-up writing assignment or in a learning journal at the end of class.
3. Specify that a number of words/terms be used in written assignments during class for section reviews, essays, or notes.
4. Encourage the use of specific words/terms in whole class or student-to-student conversation.

6 **Should we give students a sentence stem for every key concept?**

Using sentence stems is perfect for introducing concepts and for assessing student understanding during a lesson. They provide the academic language students need to communicate using new and unusual terms. When sentence stems are used consistently in the classroom, students automatically start to respond in complete sentences without reminders. The habit of reframing the language of the question into a response is a skill that students internalize through multiple practice opportunities, as well as teacher modeling.

7 **How do I write a good sentence stem?**

The easiest way to create a meaningful sentence stem is to look at the learning objectives for each lesson. What should students be able to do at the end of the lesson? Think of a question for students to answer that shows mastery of the material. Next use the academic language in the question to create a sentence stem. For example, one of the first learning objectives in most science classes is for students to know safe lab procedures. A question to ask students might be, "What are three safety procedures to use during a lab?" Using the academic language from the question, an appropriate sentence stem would be, "Three safety procedures to use during a lab are..."

Not all stems are focused on a specific content-area like the previous example. The generic sentence stems listed below can be used in any classroom or subject area.

Purpose	Stem
Summarizing	• I learned...
	• Today I realized...
	• I still wonder...
	• The most significant thing I learned today was ...
	• I would summarize my learning by saying...
	• My initial thought was ____ and now I'm thinking ____ because...
Sharing	• I feel...
	• In my opinion...
	• I predict that...
	• I agree/disagree that...
	• My view on the matter is ____ because...
	• My initial reaction is ____ because...
Justifying	• I think ____ because...
	• I agree/disagree with ____ because...
	• ____ proves that...
	• Another idea might be ____ because...
	• I was thinking that ____ should be...
	• ____ corroborates the idea that...
Accessing Prior Knowledge	• I already know ...
	• ____ reminds me of ...
	• My experience with...
	• I would like to know more about...
	• I would compare ____ to ____ because...
	• Discussing ____ made me consider...
Elaborating	• ____ is important because...
	• I chose ____ because...
	• The answer might also be ____ because...
	• I would agree or disagree with ____ because...
	• Another reason could be...
	• I would add ____ because...

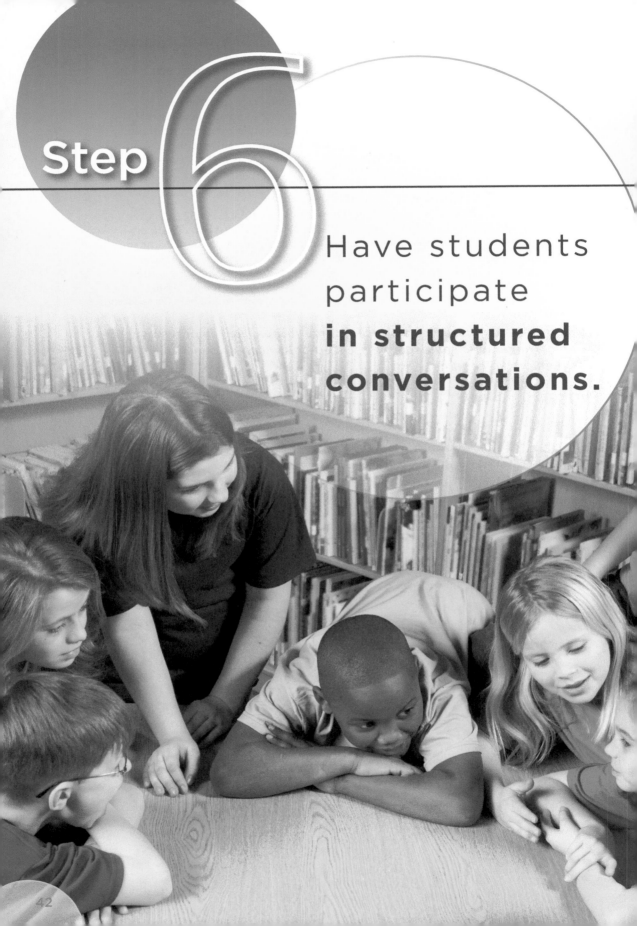

Step **6** Have students participate **in structured conversations.**

Asking students to talk with each other using specific language about a clearly defined topic is called a structured conversation. Structured conversations allow students a chance to share ideas and points-of-view with each other. When we are explicit about how students engage in discussion, it reduces a lot of the problems that arise when we ask students to work together in groups. During structured conversations, we see less off-task behavior, enhanced understanding of topic, and fewer classroom management problems.

A simple strategy that weaves structured conversation into instruction is QSSSA (Question, Signal, Stem, Share, Assess). In this strategy, the teacher asks a question and the students give a response signal when they are ready to answer. Using a sentence stem, students are asked to share their responses with one or more peers. Lastly, the teacher assesses the quality of the discussion by selecting a few students to share their answers with the whole class. Students could also share by writing and then by reading their responses.

QSSSA Template

QUESTION SIGNAL STEM SHARE ASSESS	**Simple Sample:**

Simple Sample:

1. **(Question)** What effect did the explorations of Columbus have on contemporary society in Central America and the Caribbean?

2. **(Signal)** Please stand when you can finish this sentence.

3. **(Stem)** One effect of the explorations of Christopher Columbus on contemporary society in Central America and the Caribbean was...

   Wait for all students to show signal.

4. **(Share)** Beginning with a given sentence stem, students share their responses with a peer.

5. **(Assess)** The teacher randomly assesses students by calling on them individually.

Sample Signals:

Stand
Sit Down
Raise Your Right Hand
Raise Your Left Hand
Thinker's Chin

Here are some examples:

	Question	Signal	Stem	Share	Assess
Math	What are some important things to remember when factoring equations?	Raise your hand *when you can complete this sentence* ——→	The most important thing to remember when factoring equations is... because...	Share in groups of three	Randomly call on students
Social Studies	Do you support Sam Houston's position on secession?	Place your hand on your chin *when you can complete this sentence* ——→	I support/ oppose Sam Houston's position because ...	Numbered Heads Together	Randomly select groups to respond
Science	What are some unusual characteristics of annelids?	Stand up *when you can complete this sentence* ——→	The most unusual characteristic of annelids is... because...	Share in groups of two	Randomly call on students
Language Arts	Is Stanley a hero?	Put your pen down *when you can complete this sentence* ——→	Evidence that shows Stanley is/is not a hero includes ...	Share answers with several partners	Have students write their perspectives in journals

Here's how it might sound in an Algebra class:

Teacher-Student Dialogue • Algebra

Q TRIPLE S A

Teacher: What is the first step you would take to factor this equation? Please stand when you can finish this sentence: "The first step I would take to factor this equation is ..."
Teacher waits until all students stand before proceeding.

Teacher: Using the sentence stem given, turn to the person standing nearest to you and tell them your answer. If you agree with them, say, "I agree because..." If you don't agree, say, "I disagree because ..." Ok, ready, go.

Students: The first step I would take in factoring this equation is ... *Teacher waits until all students finish sharing before proceeding.*

Teacher: Okay, what is the first step you would take to factor this equation? *Teacher randomly selects a name from a stack of cards.* Chris?

Chris: The first step I would take in factoring this equation would be to put like terms together.

Teacher: Tell me more about that ...

Structured conversation can become a regular part of classroom instruction. Before setting up the structured conversation, it is important to make sure that students have enough background information and an adequate grasp of the content that will be discussed.

Sometimes, we avoid using the strategy of structured conversation because we think it will take away valuable instructional time. Structured conversations can be short, as little as thirty-five seconds or as long as five minutes if a topic really engages the students.

Here's how a structured conversation might sound in a typical classroom:

Teacher-Student Dialogue • Chemistry

QUICK Q TRIPLE S A

Teacher: What is the smallest element on the periodic table? Please raise your hand when you can finish this sentence, "The smallest element on the periodic table is ..." *Students all raise their hands.* Turn to the person next to you and say your whole sentence. If you agree with the person say, "I agree because..." If you disagree say, "I disagree because ..."

Now, turn to each other and begin sharing.

Okay, what is the smallest element on the periodic table? *Teacher randomly selects a name from a stack of cards.* Mikela?

Mikela: The smallest element on the periodic table is hydrogen.

Teacher: Thank you, Mikela.

Is there any research that shows the effect of structured conversations on student achievement?

WHAT RESEARCH SAYS

Student-to-student interaction focused on lesson concepts has been shown to have a significant effect on student achievement (Marzano, Pickering, & Pollock, 2001). In several studies, students who participated in discussions with other students about a topic showed a percentile gain of nineteen points over students who do not participate in discussions (Guzetti et al., 1993 as cited in Marzano et al., 2001).

The use of sentence stems in structured conversations provides an opportunity to increase the number of exposures to academic vocabulary following direct vocabulary instruction. Jenkins, Stein and Wysocki (1984 found that students need at least six exposures to a word before they can remember its meaning. Structured conversations ensure that students get an exposure to academic vocabulary and a chance to use new terms in an authentic context.

Step 6

FREQUENTLY ASKED QUESTIONS

1 What is the difference between "structured conversations" and simply calling on students randomly in the classroom, one student at a time?

First, structured conversations are much more engaging because the process includes 100% student participation. In single-student questioning, we select one student at a time to respond to a teacher's question while everyone else in the classroom remains passive. With structured conversations, every student must respond by completing the sentence stem given. Students demonstrate completion by responding with the signal command. (For example, "Please stand when you can finish this sentence, *One cause of the Spanish American War was...*") Once everyone has given the signal, students share their complete sentences with a partner or in groups. The process provides enough structure to get all students involved both physically and mentally. It maximizes "engagement" time in the classroom and minimizes single-student responses.

Introducing and training your students to use structured conversations such as QSSSA early in the school year will get them accustomed to the process quickly.

2 What happens if students will not participate in the structured conversations?

Initially, there may be reluctance or hesitation by some students. Keep in mind that we are nudging our students from a very well-learned pattern of passivity into something that is much more engaging. Once students understand and have success with the process, they usually enjoy it and look forward to participating in it.

For students who need extra encouragement, we simply provide the sentence stem. If need be, we give them a phrase or answer to complete the given sentence stem. Initially, we have to push and support the students as they become accustomed to structured conversations. With encouragement, support, and repetition, even our most reluctant students will soon feel comfortable and will join the process.

3 I don't understand the "A" of QSSSA?

The "A" of QSSSA stands for *assess*. The process is simple. After students have shared their completed sentence stems with a peer, the teacher can assess their responses by randomly calling on individual students. Students can share their sentence stems, or they can write about their learning experience during the structured conversation. This allows the teacher to assess responses and check student understanding. Teachers are not evaluating students; instead, they are using student responses to know whether to re-teach or to move forward with the lesson. Other assessment methods include: whole-class written responses, or numbered heads together strategy with teams of students reporting their responses to the rest of the class.

"In my opinion, the volume increased because..."

Step

7

Have students participate in **structured reading and writing activities.**

Students read and write all the time in our classes. Step Seven is about structuring these reading and writing activities so that students gain a deep understanding of content concepts. We create structure by clearly defining our purpose, our plan, and the process for each reading or writing activity.

Structured Reading Activities

All reading activities should be purpose-driven. In other words, we should be able to answer this question: Why am I having my students read this? We derive purpose from content objectives and the state standards for each subject. Therefore, aligning the reading activity with the content objective gives us a clear purpose for the assignment.

Once the purpose for the reading activity is defined, we need to make a plan. Asking, "How will I make sure my students are ready to read this?" helps the planning process. We need to decide whether students are ready to read the text independently, and if they are not, supports need to be put in place to ensure success. To prepare students to read independently, we can establish prior knowledge of the

reading assignment, scan the text for unfamiliar words, and allow students to partner-read the text.

When students read an assignment, it is good to customize the selection of a structured reading activity because the goal is to ensure student success. Specifically, we want to think about what strategies students will use to make sense of the text. Different types of texts require diverse strategies. The thinking that goes on while reading a fairy tale is very different from the thinking required when reading a word problem in math class. Here are two specific strategies that help students understand various texts:

Somebody Wanted But So

The Somebody-Wanted-But-So strategy (Macon, Bewell, & Vogt, 1991) is used during or after reading to help students understand literary elements such as conflicts and resolutions. It is also a great summarization technique for social studies, since so much of world history is based on the wants and needs of humans. Students determine the main character (somebody), his/her motivation (wanted), the main conflict (but), and the resolution to the conflict (so).

Somebody	Wanted	But	So
The Big Bad Wolf	Pigs for dinner	They hid in the brick house.	He went hungry.
Anne Frank	To hide from the Nazis	Someone turned her in.	She died in a concentration camp.

Summarization Frames

This strategy provides a way of structuring summaries of content-area text. The frames involve specific questions that help students summarize different kinds of texts. Marzano et al. (2001) and Hill and Flynn (2006) provide the following frames as examples: Narrative Frame, Topic Restriction Illustration Frame, Definition Frame, Argumentation Frame, Problem Solution Frame, and Conversation Frame. To use this strategy, we select the most appropriate frame for the assigned text. As students read the text, they answer the questions from the frame, and then use those responses to create a summary of the text.

Here is an example of a specific summarization frame:

The Topic-Restriction-Illustration Frame

This pattern is commonly found in expository material. The questions that frame the summary are:

Topic: What is the general statement or topic?

Restriction: What information does the author give that narrows or restricts the general statement or topic?

Illustration: What examples does the author give to illustrate the topic or restriction?

Text: Mammals are a group of vertebrate animals — animals with backbones. Mammals are warm-blooded, which means their body temperature is within a narrow range, despite changes in the environment. Mothers give birth to live babies, and they nourish their babies with milk. One sub-group of mammals is the marsupial group. Marsupials give birth to live young, but the babies are still underdeveloped when they are born. Baby marsupials live inside a special pouch on the mother's stomach and feed on milk supplied by her nipples. Kangaroos are one type of marsupial. They live in Australia and on nearby islands. Kangaroos use their large back legs and tails for hopping. Another marsupial is the opossum. The Virginia opossum is the only marsupial that lives in North America. Long, shiny white hair and an undercoat of soft, woolly fur cover the Virginia opossum. An opossum has 50 teeth. It sleeps during the day and hunts for food at night.

Topic-Restriction-Illustration Frame Questions:

Topic: *What is the general statement or topic?*
Mammals have backbones, are warm-blooded, and give birth to live babies that are fed with mother's milk.

Restriction: *What information does the author give that narrows or restricts the general statement or topic?*
Marsupials are one subgroup of mammals.

Illustration: *What examples does the author give to illustrate the topic or restriction?*
Kangaroos are one kind of marsupial that live in Australia. The Virginia opossum is the only marsupial that lives in North America.

Summary: *Mammals are warm-blooded animals with backbones. Mothers feed their young with milk. Marsupials are a category of mammals. Two examples of marsupials are the kangaroo and the opossum.*

Other examples of Structured Reading Activities include:

Reading Activity	Description
SQP2RS ("Squeepers")	This is a classroom reading strategy that trains students to use cognitive and metacognitive strategies to process nonfiction text. The steps are: Survey, Question, Predict, Read, Respond, and Summarize (Echevarría, Vogt, & Short, 2008).
Cornell Notes	This is a method of note taking in which paper is divided into two columns. In one large column, students take traditional notes in outline form. In the second column, students write key vocabulary terms and questions (Pauk, 2013).
Idea Bookmarks	In this activity, students take reflective notes on bookmark-sized pieces of paper. The bookmarks include quotes, observations, and words from the reading that strike the reader as interesting or effective (Samway, 2006).
Insert Method	In this activity, students read text with a partner and mark the texts with the following coding system: a "✓" to show that a concept or fact is already known, a "?" to show that a concept is confusing, a "!" to show something is new or surprising, or a "+" to show an idea or concept that is new (Echevarría, Vogt, & Short, 2008).

Structured Writing Activities

Much like reading activities, the first step in creating structured writing activities is to determine why students need to write. Specifically, we want to define how the writing task will help students gain understanding of the content objective. For example, if a science objective requires students to explain the differences between the three states of matter, the writing assignment needs to support that goal.

The second step for creating a structured writing activity is to ask, "Can my students successfully complete the writing task on their own?" If the answer is no, then supports that lead to writing independence need to be put in place. Modeling is a very effective strategy, and all students benefit from explicit modeling of the writing task. In a think-aloud strategy, we verbalize the thinking that goes on in the writer's mind while writing. This helps establish a common ground for writers and demystifies the writing process for students. Alternative strategies include establishing prior knowledge and using sentence frames. This technique reminds students about more ideas to use in writing. Providing sentence and paragraph frames gives students more language to use to begin writing. The more ideas and language students have before they begin to write, the more independent and confident they become as writers.

Lastly, we decide on a specific writing strategy, structure, or process that reinforces the content goals. Writing activities range from informal written responses on sticky notes to formal research reports with presentations.

Here are two examples of structured writing activities:

RAFT (Role, Audience, Format, Topic)

This writing strategy enables students to write from various points-of-view, using different genres, topics, and audiences. The strategy works well in all subjects, especially in Language Arts. RAFT (Fisher and Frey, 2004) is also highly engaging for students in content-area classrooms because it injects creativity into sometimes dull concepts. RAFT stands for Role (the perspective the student takes), Audience (the individuals the author is addressing), Format (type of writing that will take place, and Topic (the subject of the writing). We can select all four categories for students, or allow students to self-select some or all of them.

Some examples include:

Class	Role	Audience	Format	Topic
Language Arts	myself	classmates	narrative	summer vacation
Math	triangle	other shapes	persuasive speech	why I can't be a square
Science	Sir Isaac Newton	students	letter	laws of motion
Social Studies	Native American chief	younger tribesman	how to	survive (find food, shelter, clothing, protection)
Physical Education	fifth grader	first-grade class	list	expectations in gym

Expert Writing

This strategy involves students taking on the role of "expert" for a given topic, concept, or unit of study. An effective way to introduce this strategy is to have all students find an area in which they are already an expert (cleaning their room, irritating their siblings, making macaroni and cheese, etc.) and to complete the expert writing process with that topic before moving to academic concepts. When ready to tackle an academic topic, students brainstorm (individually or with partners) the questions that someone would ask an expert relating to their area of expertise. For example, an expert on the Civil War might be asked the following things: Who fought in the Civil War? Why were the states fighting? Who won the Civil War? During the unit of study, or individual lesson, the student makes notes about the answers to those questions. The student then writes an explanation or description of the topic or concept including all of his or her "expert knowledge." Expert writing works across all content-areas and grade levels. Including an Expert/Novice Conversation (See Appendix) during the brainstorming phase helps generate more ideas.

Other examples of Structured Writing Activities include:

Writing Activity	Description
Dialogue Journal	This is a journal that is exchanged between the student and teacher or between two or more students that focuses on academic topics. The language used in the journal should be content-focused and academic.
Letters/Editorials	During this activity, students write letters and editorials from their own point-of-view or from the point-of-view of a character in a novel, person from history, or a physical object (sun, atom, frog, etc.)
Read, Write, Pair, Share	This strategy encourages students to share their writing and ideas during interactions. Students read a text, write their thoughts using a sentence stem, pair up with another student, and share their writing.
Draw and Write	During this activity, students express knowledge of academic content by drawing and writing.

Is there any research that shows the effect of structured reading and writing activities on student achievement?

WHAT RESEARCH SAYS

Structured reading strategies are essential for creating deep comprehension of new learning. They also help to create effective processes that can be used to "cross-check" and make sense of new material. According to Marie Clay (1991), these strategies can become a process for students to use to search for meaning in their reading. In addition, reading strategies allow students the chance to engage in metacognition as they self-monitor their understanding of the text. Active instruction should include useful strategies that model what good readers do (Allington, 2002).

Structured writing strategies are tools for learners. Fountas and Pinnell (2001) state that these strategies help students to understand the structure of informational text. Working on a chart with students or having them work in pairs assures that students understand text at a deeper level.

FREQUENTLY ASKED QUESTIONS

1 Why do all the structured reading activities require students to write?

To measure the effectiveness of structured reading activities, it is important to assess student comprehension. The thinking that occurs when students read is an internal process, and in order to assess student comprehension, we must create a path for making that process visible.

Writing about the text provides a way for students to demonstrate their understanding of the reading. An alternative way to measure reading comprehension is to have students discuss what they have read. Students can discuss their reading in groups or with the teacher, using structured conversations or sentence stems. In essence, it isn't enough to ask students to read; they must read and make sense of the text. When students respond in writing or in conversation, it is easy to see what they have learned.

2 What can I do to help my struggling readers and writers achieve success during structured reading and writing activities?

We all have students who encounter difficulty in the classroom. To help these struggling students, teach with an "I do, we do, you do," mentality. This approach is a simplified way to foster student independence. Let's look at the Draw and Write structured writing activity as an example. Our first step is to explicitly model the activity (I do). The teacher draws a picture of her thinking and then writes sentences that explain or support her drawing. Next, the teacher and the students, draw a picture of their collective thinking and then interactively write sentences to clarify the picture (we do). Lastly, students draw and write independently (you do). On-level students may only need one explicit example of this technique and one shared example in order to be successful independently, whereas our struggling students may need multiple modeled examples and many practice opportunities to master the activity.

Many teachers use students' independent work time to pre-teach concepts and vocabulary for the next day's lesson. This gives struggling students additional exposure to the material they will need. Three other ways to offer support are: to provide an already completed example of the reading or writing task for students to reference; to use adapted texts –those with abbreviated language, and to maintain a dialogue journal with each student in order to identify and correct specific areas of confusion.

3 How can I incorporate these activities and get my students ready for the state assessments in reading and writing? There isn't enough time to do both.

It is easy to think of test prep and high-interest activities as mutually exclusive, but they are just the opposite. Making structured reading and writing activities an integral part of your lessons provides students with consistent opportunities to practice the same critical-thinking skills required of them on state tests.

For example, determining a character's motivation and summarizing a narrative are both common state standards. We can teach to these standards using a structured reading activity and at the same time prepare students for the state test. Whether we choose good literature or use pre-released state tests, we can incorporate the language of the test in our instruction. To measure student comprehension, we can assign a multiple-choice worksheet (like state assessments offer), or we can have students participate in a structured reading activity like the one called Somebody-Wanted-But-So. Students only have to select an answer choice to complete the multiple-choice worksheet, but they must write thoughtful, individual responses based on their understanding of the narrative for the Somebody-Wanted-But-So activity. This writing-after-reading exercise requires much higher-order thinking skills, and in the end, this kind of activity better prepares students for state tests.

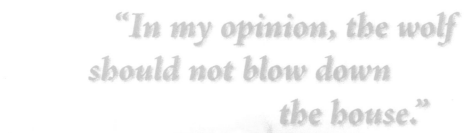

"In my opinion, the wolf should not blow down the house."

Step 6&7

with a TWIST:
Include multiple perspectives.

Why are we now going back?

After having students listen, speak, read, and write about what they are learning, we are ready to go deeper. We can now have students once again engage in structured conversation, but this time from multiple *points-of-view*. Taking on a variety of perspectives allows students to reach higher levels of thinking. This will help students develop crucial skills related to argumentative literacy. It will help them engage in meaningful discussions and use academic language to defend their ideas intelligently. There are several strategies that accomplish this goal.

Here are three examples:

T-Chart, Pair, Defend

This structured conversation allows students to approach a content concept from two opposing viewpoints.

1. Fill out a T-Chart with opposing points-of-view about a topic, as a class. For each point-of-view, write a sentence stem on the top of the column of the T-Chart.

2. Organize the students into pairs (A and B) and assign a point-of-view to each.

3. Have students use the stems and the notes taken on the T-Chart to defend their assigned point-of-view in a conversation. Students can either read the points directly off the chart or argue freely using their own words.

4. Ask a few students who used their own words to model their conversations in front of the class.

Here are some samples of possible topics and sentence starters.

Subject	Topic	Sentence Starters	
		A	B
Social Studies	Crusades	We should leave England for the Holy Land because ...	We should stay in England because ...
Science	The use of Ethanol for Energy	We must convert America to an ethanol-based economy because ...	We should not convert America to an ethanol-based economy because ...
Language Arts	*The Three Little Pigs*	The wolf should blow all the houses down because...	The wolf should not blow all the houses down because...
Math	Setting up Word Problems	We should set up a table and make a sketch before setting up these equations because ...	We should not waste time setting up a table and making a sketch before setting up these equations because...
Art	Drawing With Perspective	It's easy to draw with perspective because...	It's difficult to draw with perspective because ...

Expert/Novice

This activity is especially suited for science and math classes because students often become confused about the processes involved in various steps/procedures in these subjects.

Here are the steps:

1. Students brainstorm questions a novice might ask about a procedure or process.

2. Students list possible answers an expert might give to the questions.

3. Students form pairs (A, B). One student plays the role of a novice, and the other student is the expert.

4. Ask a few students to model their conversations in front of the class.

The expert/novice activity becomes more engaging if students can take on different roles during the activity. They can be scientists at NASA talking to tourists or math tutors from a university talking to freshmen struggling with basic concepts. For some students, playing a formal role helps them feel less inhibited. At times, we have seen the model conversations that follow this activity involve humor and style. This makes the activity memorable to the students, and these conversations help build a sense of community in the classroom.

Written Conversation

In this strategy, students pass notes back and forth.

Here are the steps:

1. Identify two points-of-view. The two perspectives do not have to be opposed to each other. For example, we might have reasons a farmer would support a tariff and reasons a businessman might support a tariff.

2. Have students brainstorm a list of key vocabulary relevant to the topic.

3. Pair the students and assign one student for each perspective. Each pair has one piece of paper.

4. Give the students a sentence starter to begin the written conversation and have them write a sentence representing their point-of-view on a piece of paper. When finished, have students pass the note to their partners.

5. Have partners read what they wrote and then write a response. Students continue to pass the note back and forth writing about their topic for ten minutes.

6. Have student notes meet the following requirements:
a. Each student writes one complete sentence each time the note is passed.
b. Sentences must have capital letters and correct punctuation.
c. Students are to use as many words as they can from the vocabulary brainstorm list or the word wall, and these words must be circled when the activity is concluded.

7. Select volunteers to read their written conversation to the class when the activity is finished.

Structured conversations from multiple perspectives are easier to facilitate if students are accustomed to the first five steps. If they know what to say instead of "I don't know," speak in complete sentences, use response signals, and use sentence stems, they are better able to participate and stay focused during the interactions.

The structured conversation format is a proven way to facilitate the use of academic language in the classroom. Also, conversations from multiple perspectives require students to use higher-level thinking skills that deepen the understanding of the concept they are studying. Structured conversations can be used as an integral part of everyday instruction.

Is there any research that shows the effect of structured conversations from multiple perspectives on student achievement?

WHAT RESEARCH SAYS

When students use the structured conversation model to defend a perspective, their emotions are engaged in an energizing and meaningful way. LeDoux (1996) found that emotions underlie the processes that create memory, meaning, and attention. Also, Marzano states that when students are asked to defend different perspectives, many new ideas are generated and concepts are understood at a deeper leve (Marzano et al., 2001).

Wiggins and McTighe (1998) define perspective as having a "critical and insightful points of view" and empathy as "the ability to get inside another person's feelings and worldview". They assert that perspective and empathy are significant factors of deep understanding of academic concepts.

1 Do we have the time to do structured conversations from multiple perspectives in the classroom?

First, let's stop and think about what we are currently doing with our students during the class period. Is it effective? What percentage of time during each class are our students engaged in learning? What percentage of time are our students thinking critically? How often do our students get the chance to verbalize and internalize the content being studied? Are students in our classrooms actively involved, or are they sitting passively?

Most of the activities listed in Step 6 & 7 with a Twist take minimal preparation and are simple to implement. Considering what is expected of our children in regard to accountability and academic growth, do we have time not to implement Step Six?

Activities which structure student conversation from multiple points-of-view provide the framework for total student engagement and foster a sense of understanding of the content both cognitively and critically. This is quality education.

2 I like the activities, but MY students will not be able to do them, will they?

Some students may initially resist some of the procedures of an interactive classroom and multiple perspective activities. Remember, we are nudging them out of their passive comfort zone into a new learning zone. If properly implemented in a well-managed environment, students will be successful with the procedures, and they will understand these procedures as a fun and successful way to learn.

On the first day of school, we should begin to nourish a climate of trust and expectation. When introduced and carefully developed, students will become accustomed to the seven steps of an interactive, language-rich classroom.

The seven steps to building a language-rich, interactive classroom provide a simple road map for the high-quality education we want our students to have. Our goal is to create classrooms where every student participates in academic conversations about great ideas. We want our students to see things from multiple points-of-view, and we want students to be able to express themselves intelligently. The rest of this chapter contains examples of twenty-five different activities that promote structured reading and writing opportunities. Also included is one extended activity called "Windows on History." It illustrates how to incorporate the seven steps during classroom instruction in order to give students a deeper understanding of the content.

These twenty-five activities provide the foundation for the kind of language-rich, interactive classroom students need.

Part 2

ACTIVITIES THAT SUPPORT STEPS 6 & 7 WITH A TWIST !

Planning Structured Conversations, Reading and Writing Activities

Which activities should you try first? Structured conversations and structured reading and writing activities can require varying degrees of teacher preparation, creativity, and interaction among students. Some teachers prefer to choose low-risk activities that are easier to manage before attempting those that involve greater degrees of spontaneous student interaction. The chart below provides a way to think about what is involved when incorporating an activity in your class. The chart is divided into the following categories:

+ Activities with minimal energy do not require a high level of face-to-

face interaction among the students. They involve whole-class discussion, questioning, and writing tasks.

+ Activities with mid-level energy involve some interaction among the students, but do not require the use of props, gestures, and materials.

+ Activities with maximum energy require students to step outside of the normal range of classroom activities and use gestures, props, humor, and character. These activities should be implemented after teachers have established a risk-free environment for students.

Minimal Energy	Mid-Level Energy	Maximum Energy
• Character Journals *p. 71*	• Artifacts and Experts *p. 66*	• Learning Styles Debate *p. 86*
• Event/Response *p. 76*	• Bystander *p. 77*	• Museum Curator *p. 68*
• Fortune/Misfortune *p. 80*	• Expert Advisors *p. 72*	• News Show *p. 74*
• Letter to the Editor *p. 88*	• Expert/Novice *p. 73*	• Prop Box Improvisation *p. 79*
• Letter/Response *p. 69*	• Freeze and Speak *p. 65*	• Slide Show *p. 67*
• Writing Windows *p. 78*	• Jury Decision *p. 84*	• Talk Show *p. 87*
• Written Conversation *p. 70*	• Perspective Choice *p. 81*	• Vocabulary Art Show *p. 75*
	• Research Team *p. 82*	
	• Supported Interview *p. 85*	
	• T-chart, Pair, Defend *p. 64*	
	• Windows on History *p. 89*	
	• Yes Conscience/No Conscience *p. 83*	

Content Areas
Language Arts,
Social Studies

Energy Level
Mid-Level

Preparation Time
15 Min.

Class Time
40 Min.
Students work in pairs
to take on the roles
of two characters in
conversation.

T CHART, PAIR, DEFEND

Description:

Preparation: The teacher prepares by selecting a content objective and a rich text that illustrates the objective. The next step is to select a pair of characters who could have a conversation, related to the text, from two different points-of-view. The teacher then identifies significant low-frequency and content area vocabulary within the text. The final step in preparing the dialogue is for the teacher to write sentence frames that incorporate some of the low-frequency and content-area vocabulary.

Delivery: When facilitating the activity with students, begin by having them read and annotate a text. Students then brainstorm possible attitudes and beliefs of both characters on a T-Chart. Encourage the students to use the vocabulary while constructing the T-Chart.

Harriet Tubman should escape because....	Harriet Tubman should not escape because...
• She knows the outdoors well and has good survival skills.	• She could be severely punished if she is caught by slave-catchers.
• She has befriended a Quaker woman who lives nearby, and she can help her get to the next station on the UGRR.	• Her husband, John, refuses to leave and she should remain with her husband.
• It is less than 90 miles to the Pennsylvania state line and Philadelphia.	• It is just too risky to try and escape alone.
• If she is sold southbound, she may never have the chance to escape again.	• She is illiterate!
• If she is successful, she might be able to help others escape also.	• Slave-catchers are everywhere, and there will be a bounty for her capture and return.
• Her cleverness will help her elude the slave-catchers.	• Her narcolepsy (sleeping spells) increases her chances of being captured.

Once the brainstorming session is complete, students then form pairs and take turns role-playing the characters in conversation. Characters could be policy-makers or scientists making a decision, historical figures, or characters from a novel or short story. The conversation always begins with a structured sentence frame. The teacher may select volunteers to perform their dialogues in front of the class and then follow with a class discussion.

There are three kinds of two-character dialogues illustrated in the sentence frames for the dialogue listed below: choice, method, and credibility.

T-Chart, Pair, Defend Dialogue Creation Guide

Opening Sentence Frames (Incorporate Vocabulary)	
1. We should/shouldn't ...	
2. The best method is ... No, I think the best method would be ...	
3. I believe/don't believe ...	

FREEZE AND SPEAK

Description:

Students engage in a dialogue representing two points-of-view in front of an audience. In mid-stream, during the conversation, the students are asked to freeze, and one individual, "frozen in dialogue," is replaced by an audience member who continues the conversation.

Freeze and Speak is an extension of T Chart, Pair, Defend with two students representing opposite points-of-view, in conversation, in front of an audience. All students should participate in T Chart, Pair, Defend prior to engaging in Freeze and Speak. Participation in T Chart, Pair, Defend will enable audience members to be prepared to replace and continue the conversation during the activity. The activity begins with two students engaging in T Chart, Pair, Defend in front of the class. The instructor then directs the students in conversation to freeze. The teacher selects one student to exit the dialogue and sit down. The teacher will then ask for a volunteer or will randomly select a student to replace the student who exited the conversation. The process continues with several students participating before the activity concludes.

Sentence Stems for Dialogue

- **We should/shouldn't ...**

- **The best method is ...**
  No, I think the best method would be ...

- **I believe/don't believe ...**

Content Area
Science, Language Arts, Social Studies

Energy Level
Mid-Level

Preparation Time
10 min.

Class Time
15 Min.
Students engage in a dialogue representing two points-of-view in front of an audience. During the conversation, the students are asked to freeze and one individual, "frozen in dialogue," is replaced by an audience member who continues the conversation.

Content Areas
Math, Science, Social Studies, Language Arts

Energy Level
Mid-Level

Preparation Time
20 Min.

Class Time
25 Min.

Students take on various roles while examining objects or texts.

ARTIFACTS AND THE EXPERTS

Description:

Before the lesson, the teacher selects an artifact that represents the topic of study. Artifacts may include items such as photographs, drawings, paintings, newspaper articles, mathematical models, tools, charts, graphs, or manipulatives.

The teacher then assigns roles to students as experts within a field of study relating to the artifact. The roles the teacher assigns depend upon the type of artifact. Some examples of possible expert roles are: biologist, historian, professor, business owner, editor, mathematician, etc. Students take on their assigned roles and write questions/observations about the artifact from their "expert" perspective. The class then discusses possible answers to some of the questions as a group.

In a math class, the teacher shows students a graph representing logarithmic growth of an investment. Students write various questions and observations about the graph from the perspective of investors.

In a science class, the teacher displays photographs and graphs showing the effects of weather changes on the migration of a bird population. Students can write various questions and observations about the photographs and graphs from the perspective of ornithologists and climatologists.

In a social studies class, the teacher shows students a photograph of a family from the depression era. Students write various questions and observations about the photographs from the perspective of historians.

Sentence Stems

- In our opinion, this is ...
- The most significant feature of this _____ is ...
- We were wondering why ...
- As _____, we were curious about ...
- One thing we noticed was ...
- We suggest ...

SLIDE SHOW

Description:

Students prepare a series of scenes in small groups depicting a sequence of events, processes, or procedures. Each group prepares a series of scenes to make one slide show. The scenes are presented through a tableaux (frozen scenes) where the students remain silent and motionless before changing to the next tableaux. Facial expressions, body stance, positioning, and minimal props support each scene. One or two students should serve as narrators to describe the events, processes, or procedures for the audience.

In a social studies class, students portray pivotal scenes of the suffragette era beginning with the 1848 Seneca Falls Convention and ending with the 19th amendment that grants women the right to vote.

In a science class, students portray the Krebs cycle by having each student take the part of a particular enzyme, co-enzyme, ATP, or ADP to represent the process.

After watching each presentation, the class reads the passage that the group used for the slide show preparation. They then discuss the various ways the group portrayed important ideas from the passage.

Content Areas
Math, Science, Social Studies, Language Arts

Energy Level
Maximum

Preparation Time
5 Min.

Class Time
45 Min.
Students create a slide show and narration to represent events, processes, or procedures.

Sentence Stems
• They demonstrated _____ by ...
• They showed how ...
• They represented the reasons why ...
• I think they were trying to show ...

MUSEUM CURATOR

Content Areas
Math, Science,
Social Studies,
Language Arts

Energy Level
Maximum

Preparation Time
20 Min.

Class Time
25 Min.
Students prepare
museum exhibits
that illustrate lesson
concepts and events.

Description:

Before the lesson, prepare descriptions of the events or concepts you wish students to illustrate in the activity. Pass out the descriptions to students in small groups, and instruct them to prepare an exhibit that illustrates the meaning of the event or concept. Each group must have one or two speakers who can explain the exhibit to visitors. Exhibits may include sculptures, tableaux, illustrations, movies, slide shows, dioramas, or machines.

For example, in a science unit about reptiles, each group is given one topic to represent. The students make products such as: a tableaux showing the extinction of reptiles, illustrations of various physical systems of reptiles, sculptures of particular reptiles, etc.

In a math class, teachers can have students create exhibits showing particular algorithms from a unit, or they can have students make exhibits modeling various word problems.

In social studies or language arts classes, teachers can have students create exhibits showing a variety of aspects of various texts and events.

When the students have finished their exhibits, they take turns wandering through the museum in groups. Half of the class can be museum visitors while the other half of the class demonstrates their exhibits.

Sentence Stems

• This exhibit illustrates the idea of...

• Our exhibit shows the events of ...

• (Event/Concept) is significant because ...

LETTER / RESPONSE

Description:

After reading and discussing a historical era, piece of literature, natural phenomenon, or organism, students select characters to whom they would like to ask particular questions. Students then write letters (individually or in partners) to the characters, objects, or organisms asking them about their lives and important decisions the individuals or objects made.

Students then exchange letters (individually or with other pairs) and write responses to the letter they received. After receiving the response, students discuss whether they agree or disagree with how the individual responded to their letters.

Content Areas
Science, Social Studies, Language Arts

Energy Level
Minimal

Preparation Time
5 Min.

Class Time
50 Min.

Students write and respond to letters written to characters, objects, or organisms.

Sentence Stems for Letter	Sentence Stems for Response
• Dear _____, I'm writing this letter to ask you about ...	• Dear _____, Thank you for your letter...
• I'm curious about why you decided to ...	• I'd like to begin by explaining why ...
• How did you feel when...	

Content Areas
Math, Science, Social
Studies, Language
Arts

Energy Level
Minimal

Preparation Time
5 Min.

Class Time
15 Min.

Students take on the
role of characters
or problem solvers
during a note-passing
activity.

WRITTEN CONVERSATION

Description:

After reading a passage or studying a phenomenon or problem, students brainstorm, as a class, the attitudes and beliefs of two characters or objects. Ask students to imagine one thing one character or object might say to the other if given a chance.

Students form partnerships, as partner "A" and partner "B." For example, in a social studies class, partner "A" might be George Washington, and partner "B" might be King George III. Partner ""A" then begins by writing a short note to partner "B." Partner "B" then reads the note, writes a response on the same paper and passes it back. This continues for ten minutes. After that time, the students discuss the note, first with each other, then with the whole class. They may read their dialogues to other groups or out loud to the class.

In a math class, students pass a note representing the views of two characters in a word problem or two different opinions on how to solve a problem.

In a science class, students take on the roles of various objects such as wind and rocks. As they do so, they discuss erosion, E-coli, or host bacteriophage.

Sentence Stems for Brainstorm	Sentence Stems for Notes
• (Character/Object) probably believes.... • (Character/Object) might say.... • One word/phrase (Character/Object) might say is....	• Dear _____, I'm writing to express my opinion about... • You might want to consider the fact that... • I must respectfully disagree with your thoughts about.... • I see we agree about ......

Rules for written conversation

a. Each person writes one complete sentence each time the note is passed.

b. Sentences must have capital letters and correct punctuation.

c. Students are to use as many words as they can from the vocabulary brainstorm list or the word wall, and these words must be circled when the activity is concluded.

CHARACTER JOURNALS

Description:

In this activity, students read a selected passage or study a particular phenomenon. Then they summarize the information as a journal entry based on the point-of-view of a character or object.

In a math class, students write a journal entry from the perspective of an individual in a word problem. For example, in a problem related to finding the perimeter of a fence, students write entries from the perspective of the fence builder who had to make decisions about finding the perimeter and building the fence.

In a science class, teachers have students write from the point-of-view of the liver describing its detoxifying role in digestion.

In a social studies class, after reading Sojourner Truth's speech entitled "Ain't I a Woman?" from the 1851 Akron, Ohio Women's Rights Convention, students respond with a character journal entry from the point-of-view of Sojourner Truth.

Content Areas
Math, Science, Social Studies, Language Arts

Energy Level
Minimal

Preparation Time
20 Min.

Class Time
25 Min.

Students write journal entries from the perspective of a character or object.

Sentence Stems

- Today I ...
- I can't believe what happened today ...
- The most amazing thing happened ...
- I will never forget ...

EXPERT ADVISORS

Content Areas
Science,
Social Studies,
Language Arts

Energy Level
Mid-Level

Preparation Time
5 min.

Class Time 55 Min. +
Students take on the
role of experts who
prepare a presentation
for someone ready
to make a significant
decision.

Description:

In this perspective-based strategy, students are required to prepare a presentation for a historical character or a person who has a pivotal decision to make.

In a science class, students assume the role of scientists who are considering whether or not to add an organism to the list of endangered species or whether or not NASA should spend money exploring the surface of Mars.

In a social studies class, students prepare a presentation for members of the Second Continental Congress on whether or not to approve Richard Henry Lee's resolution for "free and independent" colonies. The students become the "experts" regarding the topic, and in their presentations, they advise the Congress about the upcoming vote.

This strategy requires students to move to a deeper cognitive level by examining multiple points-of-view and complex details regarding the issue at hand. Students take the perspective of another time period to ultimately support their "expert" presentation and advice.

Sentence Stems

- After much consideration, it is our opinion that you should …

- One reason for our recommendation is …

- You might also want to consider the fact that …

- We took into account many factors including …

EXPERT / NOVICE

Description:

After completing a problem-solving lesson using a particular procedure students brainstorm a list of possible misconceptions and mistakes they might have made when working the problem. Students then prepare short role-plays where one student is a novice who doesn't know how to solve the problem. The other student takes on the role of an expert who will clarify misconceptions and areas of confusion. After role-playing in partners, students can then perform their role-plays in front of the class.

During the study of a lesson about moles in a science classroom, students work in pairs to play expert and novice. One student plays the role of an expert on moles and explains this animal to a student who knows little about moles.

Content Areas
Math, Science

Energy Level
Mid-Level

Preparation Time
20 Min.

Class Time
25 Min.
Students take on the role of an expert and a novice as they discuss how to solve problems.

Novice Sentence Stems	Expert Sentence Stems
• The first thing I would do is... • I understand that .... • I believe ...	• I'm afraid you're mistaken, the first step is... • I think you have a misconception; let me clarify that for you...

Content Areas
Math, Science,
Social Studies,
Language Arts

Energy Level
Maximum

Preparation Time
20 min.

Class Time
55 min. +

Students take on the
roles of producers of a
news show reporting
on a particular topic.

Description:

Students prepare a "News Show" highlighting a specific topic. The news show would include "site location," studio guest interviews, and advertisements appropriate to the topic.

In math, a unit on fractions includes interviews with: mathematicians to find out how to solve problems; people in various occupations to discover the way they use fractions in their careers; mixed numbers and improper fractions to see how they function in equations. In addition, students create advertisements using fractions or conduct on-location reports that highlight the setting of a particular word problem.

In social studies, students prepare a "News Show" regarding the nation's reaction to the Supreme Court's 1857 Dred Scott Decision. Interviews include responses from Dred Scott, members of the southern aristocracy, abolitionists such as William Lloyd Garrison and Frederick Douglass, plus President James Buchanan, as well as members of the Supreme Court.

Sentence Stems

- Good Evening Ladies and Gentlemen, welcome to ...

- We are broadcasting tonight from ...

- And now, a word from our sponsors ...

- We now go on location to ...

- Thanks _____, turning to other news ...

VOCABULARY
ART SHOW

Description:

The teacher provides vocabulary terms and definitions to groups of students. In groups, students take on the role of artists who create a visual representation of the vocabulary term. Students can create an abstract or realistic sketch or a sculpture using objects in the room. Students will select one or two representatives to be speakers who explain the visual.

When all the groups have finished, students take turns interviewing other groups about their works of art.

Content Areas
Math, Science, Social Studies, Language Arts

Energy Level
Maximum

Preparation Time
10 Min.

Class Time
25 Min.
Students become artists and reporters as they reveal the meaning and significance of words.

Sentence Stems

- **What was your term?**
- **Why did you represent it this way?**
- **I noticed how you ...**
- **I wondered why you ...**
- **Why did you decide to ...**

Content Areas
Social Studies,
Language Arts

Energy Level
Minimal

Preparation Time
20 min.

Class Time
25 Min.

Students respond to
a short story or video
clip from first-person
perspectives.

EVENT / RESPONSE

Description:

In this strategy, the teacher reads a short story aloud to the students or provides an appropriate video clip for them to preview. The reading or video clip could be from a novel, a diary entry (e.g., *The Diary of Anne Frank*), or any other grade-level appropriate literature that has appealing characters, an exciting conflict, and an intriguing plot.

After the reading or video, the teacher will lead a discussion with students to list the characters from the selection. The teacher will then assign a character to each student and ask for a written response using one of the sentence frames listed below. Students will be writing from their character's point-of-view when they respond.

The sentence frames provided for this strategy lead students to write from the first-person point-of-view. This perspective-based writing strategy fosters a deeper emotional connection to the topic and between the student and the character.

Sentence Stems

• Today I had to make a decision about...

• I survived today by...

• Let me tell you about the challenge I faced. I ...

• I can't believe what happened...

BYSTANDER

Description:

Choose a major event that took place in history, and have students read about the event in small groups. Have students brainstorm a list of important facts, ideas, and incidents that happened during the time period. In pairs, students can act as the reporter and a bystander who witnessed the event. The reporter interviews the bystander using the sentence frames listed below.

Content Areas
Social Studies, Language Arts

Energy Level
Mid-Level

Preparation Time
5 Min.

Class Time 45 Min.
Students play the role of witnesses to major historical events and take turns interviewing one another.

Sentence Stems for Brainstorm	Sentence Stems for Reporter in Dialogue
• The reporter might ask...	• We're standing here with ...
• (Character) probably believes...	• We've just learned ...
• (Character) probably observed...	• Could you tell us more about ...?
	• What were you doing when ...?

WRITING WINDOWS

Content Areas
Social Studies

Energy Level
Minimal

Preparation Time
30 min.

Class Time
60 min.

Writing Windows requires each student in a group of four to write from a particular perspective using an image as a prompt.

Description:

In groups of four, students receive a different image related to a similar topic. Each image is posted in a folder, one per folder. Students do not reveal their images to each other. In addition, students receive a 5" x 8" lined index card. All students use their index cards to respond to the following instructions:

- List everything you see in your image.

- List adjectives that would describe the objects in the image.

- Use verbs to identify the action you see in your image.

- Put your pencils down; close your eyes; step into the image and look all around. Now, open your eyes.

The teacher then says, "Now, what else do you see? List what you hear. List what you smell. List what the people are wearing and saying. Put your pencils down."

Provide each student with a second 5" x 8" lined index card featuring a prepared sentence frame prompting the student to write from a perspective within the image. For example, the four sentence frames listed below could be used with four different images of Mission San Jose. After students complete their compositions, writing is shared within the groups. After sharing, students reveal the image that inspired their writing.

Sentence Stems

- Only a few months ago, we were a nomadic band of people, and now I...

- On Sunday afternoon we hired a chauffeur and motored out to see the ruins of old Mission San Jose, and I...

- There I stood among the ruins of old Mission San Jose, ready to restore this edifice back to its majestic beauty, and I...

- I slipped away from the tour group and rounded a corner near the old convent to witness the most glorious sight, and I...

PROP BOX IMPROVISATION

Content Areas
Social Studies,
Language Arts

Energy Level
Maximum

Preparation Time
5 Min.

Class Time
30 min. preparation,
50 min. presentation.
Students use
props to create a
verbal and visual
representation of
text.

Description:

After reading and studying historical content, students use a box of props to improvise and role-play assigned scenes in history.

For example, after reading and studying the four voyages of Christopher Columbus, organize students into four teams. Each team will be responsible for developing an improvisation of one of Columbus' four westward journeys. The challenge for each team is to use as many props as possible and to incorporate as many details, low-frequency words, and content-area words as they can in the improvisation/role-play. A narrator can be chosen to narrate each presentation. Students must use at least one vocabulary word during the performance. After each presentation, debrief by asking the audience to note the content details and the effective use of props. Provide the sentence frames below for students to frame their responses.

Suggested Props for Prop Box: feathers, rope, binoculars, sunglasses, canteen, swords, scarf, artificial flowers, crosses, colored cloth fabric, markers, construction paper, bandanas, cane, crown, jewelry. (Note: swords, binoculars, crown, jewelry, etc. are all plastic and all toys.)

Sentence Stems

• They demonstrated _____ using ...

• They showed _____ with ...

• I think they were trying to show ____ using ...

• They represented ...

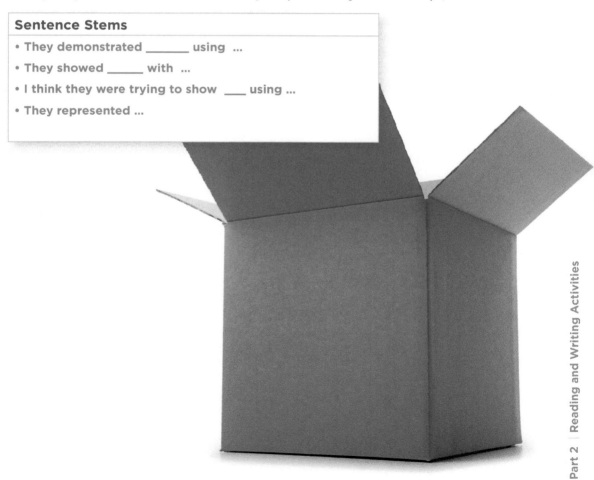

Energy Level
Minimal

Preparation Time
5 min.

Class Time 50 Min.
Students take on the role of individuals who face advantages and disadvantages due to chance events and personal choices.

FORTUNE / MISFORTUNE

Description:

This simulation enables students to experience the effects of personal decisions. Begin by reading and discussing a historical situation. Have students brainstorm a list of items they believe would be important to have if they were in that situation. For example, what would you want to have if you were a settler in Jamestown in 1607? What would you want to have if you were an American soldier in Vietnam in 1965? What equipment would you include on a mission to outer space? What tools would you need when setting up an experiment to determine weather conditions? Students then make personal choices of six to ten things from the brainstormed list of items and copy them to their notebooks.

Students then write a short paragraph from the first-person point-of-view describing that day in history. Students use the list of items as they recount this day.

Next, have the class imagine possible fortunes and misfortunes that could happen in any of the historical situations. For example, what disasters could strike Jamestown? What good things might happen to the settlers? What could happen to an American soldier during wartime conditions? What problems might happen during the course of an experiment? The teacher writes these fortunes and misfortunes on index cards.

The teacher then randomly selects a fortune or misfortune from the index cards. Students create a new paragraph to describe how they responded to the fortune or misfortune. The teacher continues drawing fortunes and misfortunes randomly. Students share their stories with a partner and then the whole class.

Brainstorm Sentence Stems	Typical Day Sentence Stems	Fortune/Misfortune Sentence Stems
• I'd want to have ... • One thing we'd need is... • _____ might be necessary to...	• Today began with ... • First, I ... • I also had a chance to ...	• It started when ... • Great news, today. • Bad news, today ...

PERSPECTIVE CHOICE

Content Areas
Social Studies,
Science,
Language Arts

Energy Level
Mid-Level

Preparation Time
5 Min.

Class Time 50 Min.
Students engage
in dialogue
from different
perspectives as they
take part in a group
of six people who
must make choices.

Description:

After reading and discussing a topic in science or social studies, select a situation in which a group of six people must make a decision. Examples include: a family of medieval peasants who are deciding whether or not to go on a pilgrimage, or a group of scientists trying to decide how to handle an epidemic.

As a class, write six different sentences that represent different perspectives on the same event using the sentence frames listed below. For example:

1. *"I think we should go on the pilgrimage because we've never been before."*

2. *"We ought to go because we will be able to visit some of the fairs and trade our goods."*

3. *"It would be a good idea to go because St. James' prayers have been known to be helpful."*

4. *"We definitely shouldn't go because I've heard towns in that area may have the plague."*

5. *"It's not wise to go because there are too many thieves along the road."*

6. *"I don't believe it's worthwhile to go because we have too much work to do here on the farm."*

Number the perspectives one through six and have students form small groups of six, each student taking a different perspective. Students begin by reading a sentence from the board and then improvising a conversation based on their impression of what the characters might say. Students may repeat their conversations as a class. The class as a whole then discusses what might be the best choice for the group.

Sentence Stems

- I think we should _____ because...

- We ought to _____ because ...

- It would be a good idea to ...

- We definitely shouldn't _____ because ...

- It's not wise to _____ because ...

- I don't believe it is worthwhile to _____ because ...

Content Areas
Science,
Social Studies,
Language Arts

Energy Level
Mid-Level

Preparation Time
30 Min.

Class Time Multiple
Class Periods

Students become
experts who research
a topic and prepare
presentations or
products based on
a social studies or
science concept.

RESEARCH TEAM

Description:

This perspective-based strategy is a long-term process, and the goal is to produce a product invented by a research team.

For example, students can be given the role of travel agents who prepare a brochure to convince their customers to travel to a particular location, or they can be scientists preparing an exhibit on endangered species for a local museum.

As an alternative, students can be given the role of World's Fair exhibition designers who research and prepare a cultural (wall panel) exhibit representing the religious, economic, social, geographic, artistic, and intellectual influences of a particular country. With multiple research teams in the classroom, several countries can be represented.

The box below provides sample directions for students.

Sample Directions

It is 1850. You have been hired as a private investigator by the United States government to research, investigate, and prepare a panel display showing the intricacies of the Underground Railroad. You are to include maps, routes, and cities that are major supply stations, individuals who are known supporters of the railroad, and other subtle codes and nuances used in this secret escape system.

YES CONSCIENCE / NO CONSCIENCE

Content Areas
Language Arts,
Social Studies

Energy Level
Mid-Level

Preparation Time
5 Min.

Class Time 30 Min.
Students have the
opportunity to
give advice to a
historical or fictional
character.

Description:

Choose a significant decision a historical or fictional character had to make. For example, during the Civil War, Harriet Tubman decided to return to Maryland to assist other slaves in their quests for freedom, and in literature, Huckleberry Finn decided to leave with Jim. As a class, think about the decisions and brainstorm reasons why the person should or should not have made the decision.

Students then form groups of three. One student in the group will take on the role of the character; the other two students will take on the role of the person's conscience. One student will try to persuade the character to make a certain decision; the other student will try to persuade the character to make the opposite decision. For example, one student will try to convince Harriet Tubman to return to Maryland; the other will try to convince her to stay in Philadelphia with her abolitionist friends.

The character making the decision can speak to the class or to their groups while they verbalize the pros and cons of the decision. After five minutes of dialogue, the character must make a decision and state the reasons for the decision. The discussions may be repeated in front of the class.

Sentence Stems Supporting (YES)	Sentence Stems Opposing (NO)	Character Sentence Stems
• You should ... • It would be wise to ... • Go ahead and...	• You shouldn't ... • It wouldn't be good to ... • The consequences of ...	• I've made my decision. I've chosen to ____ because ... • I've decided to ...

Students prepare a
case for a prosecutor
or a defendant and
then take on the role
of jurors who must
make a decision in the
case.

JURY DECISION

Description:

After studying a significant court case, have the class brainstorm arguments in favor of the defense and arguments in favor of the prosecution. Divide the class in two and ask half of the students to write a closing argument in favor of the defense and half of the class to write a closing argument in favor of the prosecution.

Divide the class into groups of six. Each group of six will consist of three students who wrote closing arguments for the defense and three for the prosecution. The same students who wrote the arguments in favor of the defense and prosecution now sit in a circle and take on the role of jurors. They must try to come to consensus about the case within a given period of time. Students can use the sentence frames below as they prepare their responses.

Debrief the activity as a class.

Prosecution Stems	Defense Stems	Juror Stems
• You should find the defendant guilty because... • The evidence shows ...	• You should find the defendant innocent because ... • The evidence shows ...	• I think the defendant is guilty/innocent because ... • The prosecution/ defense clearly proved ...

SUPPORTED INTERVIEW

Content Areas
Language Arts,
Social Studies

Energy Level
Mid-Level

Preparation Time
5 Min.

Class Time 25 Min.
Students take on the
role of historical or
fictional characters
who have made
decisions in history
or in literature. The
decision-making
process becomes
evident as they
verbalize their
thoughts in class.

Description:

Begin by choosing one historical or fictional character who has made a significant decision during the course of events in history or literature. Have students brainstorm a list of reasons they think the character used in order to make the decision. Then have students list as much information as possible about the character's life using information from textbooks, notes, or other available resources.

Choose a student to play the role of the historical/fictional character. The character can sit in the front of the classroom with three students behind him/her. The students behind the character are a visual representation of the character's mind. The student playing the character can ask questions to his "mind's eye" at any time during the interview. Additionally, the students playing the mind's eye can stop the interview and talk with the character at any time.

The rest of the class is the audience and represents characters from history/literature. The audience could be a group of reporters, soldiers, townspeople, etc. For example, a president might address the press core, George Washington might address a group of soldiers, or the magistrate in Verona might decide how to resolve the conflict between the Montagues and the Capulets. The audience will interview the character who sits in front of the classroom. The audience may only react to what they hear the character say directly to them (Wilhelm, 2002). They cannot react to anything said by the mind's eye.

Students taking part in the audience or students posing as characters can use these sentence frames:

Audience Question Stems	Character Response Stems
• My question is … • What's your view of … • Can you explain why … • Clarify your position on …	• Allow me a moment to respond to… • My opinion is … • In response to your question, I think …

Content Areas
Social Studies,
Language Arts

Energy Level
Maximum

Preparation Time
30 Min.

Class Time 55 min.
Students participate
actively in a debate
as speechwriters,
editorial writers,
political cartoonists,
and propagandists.

DEBATE

Description:

This strategy helps students prepare to debate two opposing points-of-view. Write some pro/con debates on the board, e.g., the American Revolution, the Texas Revolution, or the Civil War. Have students make a list of reasons for and against each argument.

Prepare the following signs for the classroom and display them in different corners of the room: CHEERS, EDITORIALS, CARTOONS, and SPEECHES.

Ask students to choose one of these activities (cheer, editorial, cartoon, or speech) and stand by the corresponding sign. Now have students count off as ones and twos at each station around the room. Make sure that each station has both ones and twos in order to represent all activities during the debate. Students can use their lists of reasons to prepare cheers, editorials, cartoons, or speeches that represent their points-of-view.

During the debate presentation, all the ones and twos form separate teams facing each other. The debate occurs in this order: CHEERS, CARTOONS, EDITORIALS, and SPEECHES. (Have students repeat the cheer after the cartoon, the editorial, and the speech.

After the debate, students participate in a secret ballot to determine which team won the debate.

TALK SHOW

Content Areas
Science, Social Studies, Language Arts

Energy Level
Maximum

Preparation Time
10 Min.

Class Time
55 Min.

Students participate in a talk show where they represent the views of various historical/literary characters or a scientific phenomenon.

Description:

Choose a topic for a series of talk shows that students can perform in groups. For example, if studying the causes of the American Civil War in social studies, students can choose from: "Plantation Life," "Abolitionism," "To Fight or Not to Fight?" "States' Rights," or "Lincoln, Yes or No?" A biology class might choose from these topics: "To Evolve or Not to Evolve: Single Celled Organisms Debate Their Future" or "Global Warming: Time for Decision."

In small groups, students can prepare an improvised talk show about their topic. They must choose a host, identify characters, prepare questions to ask, and write possible responses. The group can choose to allow audience questions if they wish. Students are encouraged to use humor and surprise but to avoid anachronisms.

Host Sentence Stems

• Ladies and Gentlemen, welcome to ....

• Our topic today is ...

• We have _____ with us ...

• Now, for our first question ...

• The last question for our guests is ...

LETTER TO THE EDITOR

Content Areas
Social Studies,
Science,
Language Arts

Energy Level
Minimal

Preparation Time
5 min.

Class Time 50 Min.

Students write
and respond to
editorials from the
perspective of various
historical characters
or individuals with
perspectives on
contemporary science
and social studies
topics.

Description:

Choose a controversial topic that aligns with your lesson objectives. As a class, list various perspectives on the topic and then brainstorm reasons to support each perspective.

Have students use their lists to write a letter to the editor of a newspaper reflecting their points-of-view. When complete, have the students exchange letters with a partner. Ask students to read each other's letters and then write a letter opposing what they have read.

Letter Sentence Stems	Response Sentence Stems
• Dear Editor, I'm writing concerning ...	• Dear Editor, In response to yesterday's letter concerning ...
• It is my contention that ...	• The writer said ...
• We must remember ...	• I disagree. It seems that ...
• Finally, everyone must agree that ...	• Have we not forgotten ...?

WINDOWS ON HISTORY (UNIT OF STUDY)

Description:

Teacher Preparation and Steps:

1. Select an image of a historical event (on PowerPoint or transparency).

2. Choose an image of a historical individual involved in the event.

3. Select textual information about the historical figure.

4. Reproduce the History Scene Investigation (HSI) Uncover the Picture Template (see page 91) for each student.

5. Copy the T-Chart with sentence stems for students.

6. Provide the Transition Words chart to students.

Step 1: HSI (History Scene Investigation)

- Select an image of a historical event and make a PowerPoint or transparency. Cover the image at first.

- Uncover portions of the image a little at a time. As the image is slowly revealed, students can list what they see using the HSI Uncover the Picture Template.

- Give students three opportunities during this step to predict what the image might be. Ask, "What do you think this is?" "Why do you think that?"

- Finally, reveal the entire image.

Step 2: Brainstorm Feeling Words

- Ask students to view the image carefully and to think about what emotions the people in the image must have had. Students can brainstorm a list of "feeling" words individually or as a whole group.

- Record the feeling words on chart paper.

Step 3: The Portrait Image

- Present an image of a historical figure related in some way to the image seen in Step 1. Tell students they will be reading more about this individual in a reading passage/text/content/ story. Provide this information for students before Step 4.

Step 4: Scan and Read the Text

- Students scan the text from the bottom to the top to find unfamiliar words.

- The teacher records the scan words on chart paper.

- The teacher quickly defines each term to facilitate student comprehension.

- Students read the text about the historical figure silently.

Content Areas
Social Studies, Language Arts

Energy Level
Mid-Level

Preparation Time
30 Min.

Class Time Multiple Class Periods

Students examine historical images, speak and write from multiple perspectives, and share their writing in order to gain deeper understanding of a broad content concept.

Step 5: Speaker/Leader Discussion

+ Prepare a T-Chart and brainstorm two perspectives about the historical figure and the decision he/she has to make. For example:

Harriet Tubman SHOULD run away because...	Harriet Tubman SHOULD NOT run away because...

+ Discuss possible reasons the historical figure must use to make a decision, and record the reasons on the T-Chart.

+ Divide students into pairs. Within the pairs, Student A is the Speaker, and Student B is the Leader.

+ Explain the procedure for the discussion.

Procedure:

1. The speaker begins by defending one point-of-view using the sentence stem at the top of the T-Chart.

2. The leader claps at the end of a speaker's sentence to signal the speaker to use a transition word.

3. The speaker begins to defend the opposing point-of-view from the T-Chart using a transition word.

4. The leader may clap up to 3 times.

5. The speaker/leader roles switch after one minute.

6. Repeat Steps 1-4. (adapted from Zwiers, 2008)

+ Explain that the speaker has to give reasons in support of point-of-view using the sentence stem at the top of the T-Chart. Be sure that speakers know they must include at least three scan words in their argument.

+ Describe the way the leader decides when the speaker must use a transition word to support the opposing point-of-view. (Speakers can use the Transition Words chart on this page.)

> **Transition Words**
>
> However,
>
> On the other hand,
>
> On the contrary,
>
> Yet,

Step 6: Analyze the HSI Image

+ Refer students to the HSI image.

+ Ask students to step into the image and make lists after reading the questions below. Tell students they can use words or phrases to create their lists.
    - What do you see?   - What do you smell?
    - What do you hear?   - What are the people wearing?
    - What are the people saying?

Step 7: Write and Share a Historical Narrative

• Students will describe the image using the first-person point-of-view.

• Students must include at least three scan words in their writing.

• Students will use a sentence stem provided for them. For example, "Cold, wet, and shaken, we stumbled through the night until…"

• Students share their writing with a partner when finished.

Step 8: Change the Point-of-view for a Historical Narrative (optional)

• Ask students to return to their writing and rewrite it using the third-person point-of-view. This adds a different perspective to the historical narrative.

Step 9: Write a Letter

• Have students write a letter to the historical figure including the following four elements:

   a. Tell a little about yourself.

   b. Tell the historical figure what qualities you admire about them.

   c. Ask for additional information about them.

   d. Tell them what you have in common.

Step 10: Share Letters

• Students read their letters in pairs, groups, or with the entire class.

HSI - Scene Investigation
Data Collection Sheet | Uncover the Picture Template

The Evidence	The Predictions
What do you see? List -	What do you think this is? First Prediction: I think…
	Second Prediction: Now I think…
	Third Prediction: I think…

APPENDIX 1

How to Write a Content Objective

A content objective is a clear statement that explains what students will learn or be able to do by the end of each lesson. Content objectives are the basis for all teaching and learning in the classroom. They explain which key idea or concept is the focus of instruction and at what depth students will learn it. State and district curriculum standards provide a concrete framework for teachers to decide what information to teach. Bloom's Taxonomy provides language that explains how deeply the material is taught. Effective content objectives have three characteristics: they correspond with state/district curriculum standards; they match one level of Bloom's Taxonomy; and they are measurable. Follow the step-by-step process below to write a content objective that meets all of these characteristics.

- **Knowledge:** Remembering Key concepts
  Sample verbs: define, name
- **Comprehension:** Explaining the meaning of key concepts
  Sample verbs: explain, summarize
- **Application:** Using key concepts in a new way
  Sample verbs: apply, dramatize
- **Analysis:** Breaking down the key concept into smaller parts
  Sample verbs: compare, classify
- **Synthesis:** Putting parts together to form a new idea
  Sample verbs: construct, design
- **Evaluation:** Making judgments about the key concept
  Sample verbs: assess, defend

Step One: Identify the key idea or concept to be taught.

Look at the state or district curriculum standards for the grade level and subject area being taught. Use those standards to determine the key idea or concept to teach. Many districts also have a pacing guide or scope and sequence that helps teachers decide the order in which to teach concepts.

Step Two: Determine the level of depth of understanding.

Teachers determine how in depth they want students to learn the key concept and then select a verb that matches that level of depth. For example, during introductory lessons, teachers simply want students to identify basic concepts, and in later lessons, they may want students to apply and evaluate the new concepts. Bloom's Taxonomy (in the next column) provides a leveled structure to label the depth of learning.

Step Three: Select appropriate activity(ies).

Decide what students will do in order to show that they have learned the key idea. What activity, strategy, or task will students tackle during the lesson to help them understand the key concept? This activity should be observable and measurable, that is, the student will show that he/she understands the concept. For example, "Identify the main idea and three details found in chapter seven," is observable or measurable, whereas, "Learn about the main idea and detail," is not.

Step Four: Write the content objective.

Write a complete sentence that tells the students:
1. the key concept they are going to learn.
2. the level of depth of understanding.
3. the activity(ies) they will complete.

Content Objective Checklist:

1. Does it focus on a state/district curriculum standard?

2. Does the verb in the content objective match the appropriate level of Bloom's Taxonomy?

3. Can I measure it? What will students do in order to show they are meeting the objective?

Sample verbs to include in content objectives:

Knowledge	Comprehension	Application	Analysis	Synthesis	Evaluation
Count	Classify	Act	Break down	Adapt	Appraise
Define	Cite	Articulate	Characterize	Collaborate	Argue
Describe	Conclude	Assess	Classify	Combine	Assess
Draw	Convert	Change	Compare	Communicate	Choose
Enumerate	Describe	Chart	Contrast	Compile	Conclude
Find	Discuss	Choose	Correlate	Compose	Criticize
Identify	Estimate	Collect	Debate	Construct	Critique
Label	Explain	Compute	Deduce	Create	Decide
List	Generalize	Construct	Diagram	Design	Defend
Match	Give	Contribute	Differentiate	Develop	Evaluate
Name	examples	Determine	Discriminate	Devise	Interpret
Quote	Illustrate	Develop	Distinguish	Facilitate	Judge
Read	Interpret	Discover	Examine	Formulate	Justify
Recall	Locate	Dramatize	Focus	Generate	Predict
Recite	Make sense	Draw	Illustrate	Individualize	Prioritize
Record	of	Extend	Infer	Initiate	Prove
Reproduce	Paraphrase	Implement	Limit	Integrate	Rank
Select	Predict	Interview	Outline	Invent	Rate
Sequence	Report	Include	Point out	Make up	Support
State	Restate	Inform	Prioritize	Model	Validate
Tell	Review	Instruct	Recognize	Modify	
View	Summarize	Participate	Research	Negotiate	
Write	Trace	Predict	Relate	Organize	
		Prepare	Separate	Perform	
		Produce	Subdivide	Plan	
		Provide		Produce	
		Relate		Propose	
		Report		Rearrange	
		Select		Revise	
		Show		Rewrite	
		Solve		Substitute	
		Transfer			
		Utilize			

Examples for How to Write a Content Objective

First Grade Language Arts

Step One: Identify the key idea or concept.	To decode words in context and in isolation by applying common letter-sound correspondences, including long E. (State Standard)
Step Two: Determine level of depth of understanding.	Identify (Knowledge level of Bloom's Taxonomy)
Step Three: Select appropriate activity(ies).	Point to long E words while listening to *Brown Bear, Brown Bear, What Do You See?*
Step Four: Write the content objective.	Students will be able to identify words with the long E spelling by pointing to them as they listen to *Brown Bear, Brown Bear, What Do You See?* (State Standard)

Eighth Grade Math

Step One: Identify the key idea or concept.	To select and use appropriate operations to solve problems and justify solutions. (State Standard)
Step Two: Determine level of depth of understanding.	Apply (Application level of Bloom's Taxonomy)
Step Three: Select appropriate activity(ies).	Solve multistep word problems involving everyday activities.
Step Four: Write the content objective.	Students will be able to apply addition, subtraction, multiplication, and division skills to solve multistep word problems involving everyday activities. (State Standard)

Fifth Grade Social Studies

Step One: Identify the key idea or concept.	To explain the reasons for and rights provided by the 15th amendment to the U.S. Constitution. (State Standard)
Step Two: Determine level of depth of understanding.	Articulate (Application level of Bloom's Taxonomy)
Step Three: Select appropriate activity(ies).	Create a news show in groups of three.
Step Four: Write the content objective.	Students will be able to articulate the reasons for and rights provided by the 15th amendment to the U.S. Constitution by creating a news show in groups of three. (State Standard)

Biology

Step One: Identify the key idea or concept.	To compare and contrast prokaryotic and eukaryotic cells. (State Standard)
Step Two: Determine level of depth of understanding.	Compare and contrast (Analysis level of Bloom's Taxonomy)
Step Three: Select appropriate activity(ies).	Complete a Venn Diagram.
Step Four: Write the content objective.	Students will be able to compare and contrast prokaryotic and eukaryotic cells by completing a Venn Diagram. (State Standard)

Sixth Grade Language Arts

Step One: Identify the key idea or concept.	To include dialogue that develops the plot in imaginative stories (State Standard)
Step Two: Determine level of depth of understanding.	Include (Application level of Bloom's Taxonomy)
Step Three: Select appropriate activity(ies).	Write two sentences using dialogue.
Step Four: Write the content objective.	Students will be able to include two sentences of dialogue to develop the plot in an imaginative story. (State Standard)

APPENDIX 2

How to Write a Language Objective

A language objective is a clear statement that explains what language skills or processes students will use during a lesson. Many teachers of English Language Learners have used language objectives as a way to focus language development for their students. Language objectives communicate the specific ways that students will listen, speak, read, or write. Each state's English Language Development/English Language Proficiency (ELD/ELP) standards can provide a concrete framework for writing language objectives. Effective language objectives have three characteristics: they support the lesson's content; they match English Language Development/ English Language Proficiency (ELD/ELP) standards; and they are measurable.

Here are some examples of language objectives written for real classrooms:

Content Objective	Language Objective
Students will be able to explain the reasons for the rights provided by the 15th amendment to the U.S. Constitution.	Students will speak using a variety of sentence stems to explain the reasons for the adoption of the 15th amendment as they use the words ratify and citizenship.
Students will be able to compare and contrast prokaryotic and eukaryotic cells.	Students will be able to compare/contrast cells on a Venn diagram.
Students will be able to apply addition, subtraction, multiplication, and division skills to solve an original multistep word problem, involving an everyday activity.	Students will be able to write a multistep word problem using the words: *best represents, total amount*, and *least to greatest*.
Students will be able to identify and use dialogue.	Students will be able to construct two sentences of dialogue in an imaginative story.

The following chart lists examples of language objective starters:

Language Objectives Aligned to Cross-Curricular Student Expectations

Listening	Speaking
• Recognize correct pronunciation of .... • Recognize sounds used in the words _____ and ... • Identify words and phrases heard in a discussion about ... • Check for understanding by ..../Seek help by ... • Use ___ (media source) to learn/review .... • Describe general meaning, main points, and details heard in ... • Identify implicit ideas and information heard in ... • Demonstrate listening comprehension by... • Identify relationships between sounds and letters by...	• Pronounce the words ____ correctly. • Use new vocabulary about ____ in stories, pictures, descriptions, and/or classroom communication ... • Speak using a variety of sentence stems about ... • Speak using the words____ and ___ about... • Share in cooperative groups about ... • Ask and give information using the words _____ and... • Express opinions, ideas, and feelings about ___ using the words/phrases... • Narrate, describe, and explain .... • Use formal/informal English to say ... • Respond orally to information from a variety of media sources about...
Reading	**Writing**
• Recognize directionality of English text. • Recognize the words/phrases _____ and .... • Use prereading supports such as____ to understand ... • Read materials about ___ with support of simplified text/visuals/word banks as needed. • Use visual and contextual supports to read ... • Show comprehension of English text about ... • Demonstrate comprehension of text read silently by... • Show comprehension of text about ___ through basic reading skills such as ... • Show comprehension of text/graphic sources about ___ through inferential skills such as ... • Show comprehension of text about ___ through analytical skills such as ...	• Learn relationships between sounds and letters when writing about ... • Write, using newly acquired vocabulary, about... • Spell English words such as _____ and ... • Edit writing about ... • Use simple and complex sentences to write about ... • Write using a variety of sentence frames and selected vocabulary about ... • Narrate, describe, and explain, in writing, about ...

APPENDIX 3

TIPS
Principles for a Language-Rich Interactive Classroom

The Seven Steps are based on four key ideas, or TIPS, that lay the groundwork for a successful language-rich, interactive classroom.

Total Participation

This principle is clear: ALL students must participate. This means that every student, during every activity, is involved in listening, writing, speaking, or reading. The type of participation may vary from student to student depending on his or her ability and the task at hand, but non-participation is not an option in a language-rich, interactive classroom. The key to securing 100% participation from our students is to create an environment where students want to be involved. Some easy ways to begin total participation include: greeting each student warmly, incorporating student interests in lessons, and decorating the classroom with student work. When students know that teachers care about them and want to teach in a way they understand, even the most reluctant learners begin to participate.

Incorporate Academic Vocabulary

The vocabulary used within most classrooms is largely centered on specific content concepts. Our goal is to have students learn and use academic vocabulary in each lesson in clear and effective ways. For example, we want students in science class to use science vocabulary in the proper context when speaking and writing. While it can be difficult to determine which words to teach, especially if our students begin with limited vocabulary knowledge, there are methods to use. Thinking about academic vocabulary in terms of Brick and Mortar words can guide us.

Brick words are content specific vocabulary. In seventh grade math class, for example, some brick words are: three-dimensional, polygon, and prism. Brick words for second grade social studies class might include: natural resource, producer, and consumer. These words are found in the glossary of a content textbook, but it is up to teachers to teach brick words explicitly using vocabulary strategies like word webbing, the Frayer Model, and personal dictionaries.

Mortar words are academic words that connect, describe, or help us process the brick words. Mortar words are not found in any glossary, but textbooks and tests use these words regularly. Examples of mortar words are: similar, between, finally, disagree, possibility, and based upon. We do not need to teach the meaning of these words explicitly, but we need to increase student comprehension of mortar words by simply using them as part of our conversations. Instead of asking a student, "What do you think about what you just read?", reframe the question using mortar words and ask, "Based upon the passage, what is your opinion of what you just read?" The more students hear academic language, the more they will use it. Repetition is the key.

Promote Literacy and Language Development

During both planning and executing lessons, we have a goal that is two-fold: build literacy for students while developing their academic language skills. Literacy refers to student understanding of the important ideas, the key concepts of any given content-area (subject), and the ability to use new material in effective ways. In order to promote content literacy for students, we make the material easy to understand. Then we provide multiple opportunities for students to interact with the material using critical thinking skills like evaluating, generalizing, and classifying information. While building content literacy, we develop students' academic language skills. To promote language development, we create time for students to listen, speak, read, and write about the content in every lesson.

Support for Struggling Learners

Some learners struggle with a specific concept in one subject; other learners, like beginning ELLs, may face an ongoing, comprehensive struggle in all subjects. Either way, the goal is to provide support that gives students the self-confidence and independence they need to succeed. Being prepared to help struggling learners who encounter difficulty means examining our learning environment as well as our classroom procedures. In our classrooms, we can create supportive environments by filling the walls with visuals that are teaching tools, by arranging desks so that students can collaborate, and by teaching students how to use resources within the classroom. During instruction, we can model what to do when students get stuck, and we can encourage students to use a buddy for clarification. In addition, teaching students to use problem-solving skills will diminish the struggle some students have and make it easier for them to learn.

When we plan instruction using TIPS as a guide, our students benefit. By creating lessons that involve total student participation, incorporate academic vocabulary, promote literacy and language, and support struggling students, we establish a framework for success. Using the seven steps and the TIPS framework, we have the tools to insure that our students are involved, articulate, and successful.

APPENDIX 4

Guide to Terms and Activities

The terms and activities listed below provide an additional resource for teachers who want to increase student engagement and achievement in their classrooms. Included in the list is a brief description of the activity and a citation for additional information for each activity. Becoming familiar with the terms and implementing the activities with students will transform any classroom into a language-rich interactive classroom.

Accountable Conversation Questions:
Place the following poster in your room:

What to Say
Instead of I Don't Know
- **May I please have some more information?**
- **May I please have some time to think?**
- **Would you please repeat the question?**
- **Where could I find more information about that?**
- **May I ask a friend for help?**

Model the way students can use the poster questions when they are unsure about what to say when called on by the teacher (Seidlitz & Perryman, 2008). Students should know that they can either respond, or ask for help and then respond when the teacher calls on them. Newcomer English Language Learners should not be pressured to speak in front of the class if they have not yet begun to show early production levels of speech proficiency. Students should be encouraged, but not forced to speak when in the silent period of language development (Krashen, 1982).

Academic language: Academic language is specialized vocabulary. Its structures tend to be more abstract, complex, and challenging and are found with high frequency in classroom oral and written discourse.

Adapted Text: Adaptations in text helps struggling students comprehend academic language. Some methods include: graphic organizers, outlines, highlighted text, taped text, margin notes, native language texts, native language glossaries, and word lists (Echevarria, Vogt, & Short, 2008).

Advance Organizers: Information given prior to reading or instruction helps students organize information they encounter during instruction (Mayer, 2004). Advance organizers should activate prior knowledge and help organize new information. Examples include: graphic organizers, anticipation guides, KWL, guided notes, etc.

Affective Filter: This is the emotional barrier to language acquisition caused by a negative perception or response to one's environment.

Anticipation Chat: Prior to instruction, a teacher facilitates a conversation between students about the content to be learned. The teacher opens the discussion by having students make inferences about what they are going to learn based on prior knowledge, experiences, and limited information about the new concepts (Zwiers, 2008).

Anticipation Guides: This is a structured series of statements given to students before instruction. Students choose to agree or disagree with the statements either individually or in groups. After instruction, students revisit the statements to discuss whether they have changed their minds about the statements. New learning can often inform and change student opinion (Head & Readence, 1986).

Backwards Book Walk: Students scan a nonfiction text, briefly looking at headings, illustrations, captions, key words, and other text features before reading a book. After the scan, students discuss what they believe they will learn from the text (Echevarria, Vogt, & Short, 2008).

Book Reviews: Students read and examine book reviews. After being immersed in the book review genre, English Language Learners write short reviews which can be published for others to read (Samway, 2006).

Brick Words: Brick words are content specific vocabulary (Dutro & Moran, 2003).

Brick and Mortar Cards: Students are given five "brick" cards with academic vocabulary (content area terms) and are instructed to organize them in a way they think makes sense. Afterward, they have to link the cards together using "mortar" words. Mortar words tie the language together. Students may need lists of sentence terms and connecting words to facilitate the process (Zwiers, 2008).

CALLA Approach (Cognitive Academic Language Learning Approach): This approach to teaching English Language Learners requires explicit instruction in language learning strategies, academic content, and language skills through scaffolding, active engaged learning, and language use (Chamot & O'Malley, 1994).

CCAP (Communicative Cognitive Approach to Pronunciation): This five step process helps English Language Learners improve pronunciation skills (Celce-Murcia, Brinton, & Goodwin, 1996 as cited in Flores, 1998). The steps include the following:

- Description and analysis of the pronunciation feature
- Listening/discrimination activities (See Segmental/Supra-Segmental Practice in this guide.)
- Controlled practice and feedback
- Guided practice and feedback
- Communicative practice

Canned Questions: Students are given a series of question stems ranging from the lowest to the highest level of Bloom's Taxonomy in order to participate in discussions about a topic. For example:

- "What is…"
- "How do…"
- "What would be a better approach to…"
- "How do you know that…"

(Echevarria, Vogt, & Short, 2008)

Card Sort: In this activity, students are given a set of cards with pictures and/or words and asked to sort them into categories. Sample categories resemble the following: living vs. nonliving, states of matter, types of energy, etc. While students are sorting the cards, they ask their group members questions like:

- What does this picture show?
- What category would be good for this card?
- How can we be sure these cards all go together?
- Which rule are we using to categorize this card?

Carousel Activity: In this activity, groups are assigned to stations in the classroom. Each station has a set of questions, and students are given a specified time to answer the questions. Groups rotate from station to station until they have answered all questions. This activity encourages interaction among students.

Chat Room: In this writing activity, students use informal and formal English to describe terms and concepts. Each student is given a paper outline of a computer screen and a term or concept. On the computer screen, students describe the term or concept by writing a text message using informal English. Students then switch computer screens with a partner. The partners rewrite the text message using formal English.

Choose the Words: During this activity, students select words from a word wall or word list to use in a conversation or in writing.

Chunking Input: Chunking means to break-up material into smaller units for easier comprehension. Visual and auditory information can be chunked so that students have time to discuss new information, pay attention to details, and create schema for organizing new information.

Cloze Sentences: Fill-in-the-blank sentences help students process academic text (Taylor, 1953; Gibbons, 2002).

Compare, Contrast, Analogy, Metaphor, and Simile Frames: These sentence frames help students organize schema for new words (Marzano et al., 2001; Hill & Flynn, 2006).

For example:

+ Compare: ____ is similar to ____ in that both....
+ Contrast: ____ is different from ____ in that ...
+ Analogy: ____ is to ____ as ____ is to ____
+ Metaphor: I think _____ is.....
+ Simile: I think ____ is like/as... because...

Comprehension Strategies: Comprehension strategies help proficient readers understand what they read. These strategies can be used for different kinds of text, and when they are taught, students are more likely to use them. Strategies include: prediction, self-questioning, monitoring, note-taking, determining importance, and summarizing (Echevarria, Vogt, & Short, 2008; Dole, Duffy, Roehler, & Pearson, 1991; Baker, & Boonkit 2004).

Concept Attainment: This Jerome Bruner strategy instructs teachers to provide examples and non-examples of concepts to students. Then teachers can ask students to categorize the examples. Over time, students learn to categorize at increasing levels of depth and understanding (Boulware & Crow, 2008; Bruner, 1967).

Concept Definition Map: This visual organizer enables students to process a term. (Echevarria, Vogt, & Short, 2008.) Four questions are asked:

+ What is the term?
+ What is it?
+ What is it like?
+ What are some examples?

Concept Mapping: This is a technique for making a visual diagram of the relationship between concepts. Concept maps begin with a single concept written in a square or circle in the center of a page. New concepts are listed and connected with lines and shapes creating a web that shows the relationship between the ideas (Novak, 1995).

Conga Line: During this activity, students form two lines facing one another. Students in each line share ideas, review concepts, or ask one another questions. After the first discussion, one line moves and the other remains stationary so that each student can converse with a new partner (Echevarria, Vogt, & Short, 2008).

Content-Specific Stems: In this activity, sentence stems using content specific vocabulary are provided to students. For example, instead of a general stem such as, "In my opinion...," a content specific stem would be, "In my opinion the Declaration of Independence is significant because..."

Contextualized Grammar Instruction: Teaching grammar in mini-lessons demonstrates specific, meaningful tasks that students can transfer to writing or speaking. The purpose of the grammar instruction is to enable students to communicate verbally and to write more effectively (Weaver, 1996).

Cornell Notes: Students use this method of note-taking in which a paper is divided into two uneven columns. In one large column, students take traditional notes in modified outline form. In the smaller column, students write key vocabulary terms and questions (Pauk, 2000).

Creating Analogies: This method is used to generate comparisons using the frame: _____ is to _____ as ___ is to _____ (Marzano et al., 2001).

Creating Words: This vocabulary game provides an opportunity for students to review key vocabulary by using words in creative ways. To start, a student selects a word and rolls a cube that has the following on its sides: model it, draw it, act it out, write it, talk about it, etc. Based on the outcome of the rolled cube, the student represents the word, and the classmates guess the word.

Daily Oral Language: During a five-minute mini-lesson, students view a list of sentences with incorrect English usage. Students learn correct usage by correcting the mistakes in the sentences (Vail & Papenfuss, 2000).

Dialogue Journal: A dialogue journal is exchanged between the student and teacher or between two or more students. The journal focuses on academic topics, and the language used by the teacher and student should be content focused and academic (Samway, 2006).

Direct Teaching of Affixes: During this activity, students build knowledge of English word structures by learning prefixes and suffixes (White, Sowell, & Yanagihara, 1989).

Direct Teaching of Cognates: These lessons include words that sound the same in the primary language and the target language. For a list of Spanish and English cognates, see: http://www.colorincolorado. org/pdfs/articles/cognates.pdf Students must be careful of false cognates, words that sound the same in the primary and target language, but do not have the same meaning. For a list of false Spanish/English cognates, see: http://www.platiquemos-letstalk.com/Extras/Articles/FalseCognates/FalseCongnatesMain.htm

Direct Teaching of Roots: These lessons teach the Greek and Latin roots that form the base of many English words. A partial list of roots can be found here: https://www.msu.edu/~defores1/gre/roots/gre_rts_afx2.htm

Directed Reading-Thinking Activity (DRTA): During reading, the teacher stops regularly to have students make and justify predictions. Questions might be: What do you think is going to happen? Why do you think that will happen next? Is there another possibility? What made you think that? (Echevarria, Vogt, & Short, 2008).

Directionality Sort: In this activity, students sort texts in various languages on perceived directionality. Is the text written from top to bottom, then left to right? Is the text right to left, then top to bottom? Check www.newoxxo.com for newspapers that show letters and characters used in a variety of languages.

Dirty Laundry: This vocabulary activity helps students extend their knowledge of newly acquired words/terms. Students are given one vocabulary word or content concept and an outline of a paper t-shirt. On one side of the t-shirt, students write a message about their assigned word, without using the word. On the reverse side of the t-shirt, students draw a picture of the word/term. The aim of this activity is to have other students in class guess the word described on the t-shirt. T-shirts can be displayed on classroom walls or hung using clothespins (Created by Cristina Ferrari, Brownsville ISD).

Discovery Learning: This is an inquiry-based approach to instruction in which teachers create problems and dilemmas through which students construct knowledge. Ideas, hypotheses, and explanations continue to be revised while learning takes place (Bruner & Kalnins, 1967). This discovery approach has been criticized by some (Marzano et al., 2001; Kirschner, Sweller, & Clark, 2006) for teaching skills to novices who don't have adequate background and language to be able to learn new content. Teachers of English Language Learners must be careful to pre-teach content area functional language and set goals and objectives for the lesson when using the discovery approach.

APPENDIX 4

Discussion Starter Cards: Small cards containing sentence starters are given to students to use when beginning an academic conversation or when seeking ways to extend a conversation. For example: "In my opinion…", "I think…", "Another possibility is …", etc. (Thornberry, 2005).

Double Entry Journals: This is a two-column journal used for reflective writing about texts. In one column, students write words, phrases, or ideas they found interesting or significant while reading. In the other column, students write the reasons they found the words significant, or they list ways they could use them in their own writing (Samway, 2006).

Draw & Write: This exercise allows English Language Learners to express their knowledge of academic content while drawing and writing. Students may use their native language to express ideas but are encouraged to express new concepts using English (Adapted from: Samway, 2006).

Experiments/Labs: This is a form of discovery learning in science where students directly encounter the scientific process: making an observation, forming a hypothesis, testing the hypothesis, and coming to a conclusion. Teachers of English Language Learners need to make sure to pre-teach necessary content and functional vocabulary to enable full participation of ELLs.

Expert/Novice: This is a simulation involving two students. One student takes on the role of an expert and the other a novice in a particular situation. The expert responds to questions asked by the novice. The procedure can be used for lower level cognitive activities, such as having students introduce one another to classroom procedures or for higher level activities, such as explaining content area concepts in depth. The procedure can also be used to model the difference between formal and informal English, with the expert speaking formally and the novice informally (Seidlitz & Perryman, 2008).

Field Notes: Field notes are notes/reflections written in journals when studying new content. Field notes can be written or drawn and should be content focused. They can contain both social and academic language (Samway, 2006).

First-Person Narrative: When writers write from their own point of view, they are writing from the first-person. When writing in the first-person, writers use the pronoun, "I."

Flash Card Review: To engage in this exercise, students make flash cards that include definitions and illustrations of words. Students can study, play games, and sort the flash cards in various ways.

Fluency Workshop: In triads, students take turns listening and speaking to one another about the same topic. Each student has one turn to speak, while the others listen. When listening, students may ask questions, but they cannot contribute an opinion about the speaker's words. After the activity, students evaluate their level of fluency to see how levels improved from the beginning to the end of the workshop (Maurice, 1983).

Fold the Line: For this activity, students line up chronologically based on a predetermined characteristic such as height, age, number of pets, etc. Then the line folds in half upon itself, providing each student a partner. Students are then asked to formulate a response/answer to a task or question. Depending on the task/question, students use formal or informal English to share responses with partners (Kagan, 1992).

Formal/Informal Pairs: The teacher writes a statement on two strips of paper; one with formal English, one with informal English. The teacher distributes one strip to each student. Students have to find their match in the classroom.

Four Corners Vocabulary: This is a way of processing vocabulary using a paper or note card divided into four sections: term, definition, sentence, and illustration (Developed by D.Short, Center for Applied Linguistics. Described in: Echevarria, Vogt, & Short, 2008).

Framed Oral Recap: This is an oral review involving two students using sentence starters. Students are given stems such as: "Today I realized…", "Now I know….," and "The most significant thing I learned was …." Students pair up with a partner to discuss what they have learned in a lesson or unit (Adapted from Zwiers, 2008).

Free Write: During free write, students write nonstop about a topic for five to ten minutes. The goal is to keep writing, even if they can't think of new ideas. They may write, "I don't know what to write," if they are unable to think of new ideas during the free write. English Language Learners can sketch and write in their native language although they should be encouraged to write in English (Elbow, 1998).

General Stems: These are incomplete sentences that scaffold the development of language structures to provide the opportunity for conversation and writing in any academic context.

Genre Analysis/Imitation: Students read high quality selections from a genre of literature during this activity. They note particular words, phrases, and ideas they found interesting or effective and record those in a journal. Students then use their notes and observations as a resource when writing in that genre (Adapted from Samway, 2006).

Glossary Circles: This activity is based on the idea of Literature Circles (Daniels & Steineke, 2004). In this activity, students work collaboratively on a set of related terms. They are given one glossary page per term, using a template that includes four squares labeled Vocabulary Enrichment, Illustration, Connections, and Discussion Questions. During learning, students share terms, illustrations, definitions, connections, and questions that have been added to the glossary page.

Graffiti Write: In small groups, students are asked to simultaneously list academic words tied to a particular concept, within a short time frame.

Graphic Organizers: Graphic organizers are a form of nonlinguistic representation that can help students process and retain new information. They provide a way of developing a learner's schema by organizing information visually. Examples include the T-Chart, Venn diagram, Concept Map, Concept Web, Timeline, etc. (Marzano et al., 2001).

Group Response with a White Board: During this activity, students write responses to questions on white boards using dry erase markers. These can be made from card stock slipped into report covers, or with shower board cut into squares that fit on student's desks. White boards are a form of active response signal shown to be highly effective in improving achievement for struggling students.

Guess Your Corner: This activity provides a way to review/assess student comprehension of key content concepts. To begin, post four previously introduced terms/content concepts around the classroom. Give each student a characteristic, attribute picture, synonym, etc. for one of the four terms/content concepts. Students are responsible for guessing the correct concept.

Guided Notes: Teacher prepared notes used as a scaffold help students practice note-taking skills during lectures. For examples of guided note formats see: http://www.studygs.net/guidednotes.htm

Hand Motions for Connecting Words: Gestures representing transition/signal words help students visually model the function of connecting words in a sentence. For example, students might bring their hands together for terms like: also, including, as well as, etc. For terms such as excluding, neither, without, no longer, etc., students could bring their hands apart. Students can invent their own signals for various categories including: comparing, contrasting, cause and effect, sequence, description, and emphasis (Adapted from: Zwiers, 2008).

Hi-Lo Readers: While reading books are published on a variety of reading levels, they can have the same content focus and objective. For samples, see the National Geographic Explorer Books found on these web sites: http://new.ngsp.com/Products/SocialStudies/ nbspnbspNationalGeo-graphicExplorerBooks/tabid/586/Default.aspx and http://www.kidbiz3000.com/

History Scene Investigation (HSI): The teacher presents a covered image of a historical scene. The image is slowly uncovered while students make and record observations and predictions. This activity can be used as a discussion starter for a pre-writing activity (Seidlitz & Perryman, 2008).

Homophone/Homograph Sort: The teacher prepares homophone/homograph cards, listing words that sound the same, but are spelled differently, e.g., know/no, hear/here. The teacher asks the students to place the words that sound the same in groups and then to explain the meaning of each word.

Idea Bookmarks: For this activity, students take reflective notes from the books they are reading on bookmark-size pieces of paper. The bookmarks include quotes, observations, and words that strike the reader as interesting or effective. The bookmarks can be divided into boxes to add more quotes and page numbers (Samway, 2006).

IEPT (Inter-Ethno-linguistic Peer Tutoring): This research-based method increases fluency for English Language Learners by pairing them with fluent English speakers. In highly-structured tasks, fluent English speakers are trained to promote extensive interaction with English Language Learners.

Improv Read Aloud: During this exercise, students act out a story silently while the teacher or another student reads it aloud. Each student has a role to play and has to improvise the part while the story is being read. Afterward, students discuss the techniques and ideas students used to act out their part during the improv (Zwiers, 2008).

Insert Method: In this activity, students read text with a partner and mark the texts with the following coding system: a check to show a concept or fact already known, a question mark to show a concept that is confusing, an exclamation mark to show something new or surprising, or a plus to show an idea or concept that is new (Echevarria, Vogt, & Short, 2008).

Inside/Outside Circle: Students form two concentric circles facing one another, an inside circle and an outside circle. Students can then participate in a short, guided discussion or review with their partner. After the discussion, the outside circle rotates one person to the right while the inside circle remains still. All students now have a new partner. This exercise facilitates student conversations (Kagan, 1990).

Instructional Conversation: During this activity, students engage in conversation about literature through open-ended dialogue with the teacher or with students in small groups. Instructional conversations have few "known answer" questions; therefore they promote complex language and expression (Goldenberg, 1992).

Instructional Scaffolding: This model of teaching helps students achieve increasing levels of independence following the pattern: teach, model, practice, and apply (Echevarria, Vogt, & Short, 2008).

Interactive Reading Logs: Reading logs are used by students during silent reading to reflect on the text. These logs can be exchanged with other students or with the teacher for questions, comments, or responses. These logs are ideal components of an SSR program.

Interview Grids: Interview grids help students record other student's responses to various questions that express: facts, opinions, perspectives, analyses, suggestions, and hypotheses. To engage in this activity, students interview a partner in the classroom who responds to their list of questions (Zwiers, 2008). For example:

	Why are there waves in the ocean?	Why do you think some waves are higher than others?
Brian		
Enrique		
Christina		

Keep, Delete, Substitute, Select: Students learn a strategy for summarizing developed by Brown, Campoine, and Day (1981) as discussed in Classroom Instruction That Works. (Marzano et al., 2001). When using this strategy, students keep important information, delete unnecessary and redundant material, substitute general terms for specific terms (e.g. birds for robins or crows, etc.), and select or create a topic sentence. For ELLs, Hill and Flynn (2006) recommend using gestures to represent each phase of the process and to explain the difference between high frequency and low frequency terms.

KID (Keyword, Information, Drawing): In this activity, students list a word, important information about the word, and then a drawing of the word.

KIM (Key, Information, Memory Cue) Chart: This graphic organizer lets students organize what they are learning, have learned, or need to review. In the K (Key) section of the organizer, students jot down key points that are being taught or that have been learned. In the I (Information) section, students list important information that supports those points. And in the M (Memory Cue) section, students create a visual representation as a summary of what was learned (Castillo, 2007).

KWL (Know/Want to Know/Learned): This is a pre-reading strategy used to access prior knowledge and set up new learning experiences (Ogle, 1986). To begin, the teacher creates a chart where students respond to three questions: What do you know? What do you want to know? What have you learned? The first two questions are discussed prior to reading, and the third is discussed after reading. When discussing the third question, students may find they have changed their minds based on information they gathered while reading.

Language Proficiency Level: This is a measure of a student's ability to listen, speak, read, and write in English.

Learning Logs and Journals: Students can record observations and questions about what they are learning in a particular content area with learning logs or journals. The teacher can provide general or specific sentence starters to help students reflect on their learning (Samway, 2006).

Letters/Editorials: For this activity, students can write letters and editorials from their own point of view or from the point of view of a character in a novel, a person from history, or a physical object (sun, atom, frog, etc.). Teachers of ELLs should remember to scaffold the writing process by providing sentence frames, graphic organizers, wordlists, and other writing supports. Newcomers may use the Draw & Write method (see explanation above).

Linguistic Accommodations: The ways to provide access to curriculum and opportunities for language development for English Language Learners are: comprehensible input, differentiating based on language proficiency level, and scaffolding.

List/Group/Label: Students are given a list of words or students brainstorm a list of words as they engage in listing, grouping, and labeling. They sort the words on this list into similar piles and create labels for each pile. This can be done by topic (planets, stars, scientific laws, etc.) or by word type (those beginning with a particular letter, those with a particular suffix, or those in a particular tense) (Taba, 1967).

List Stressed Words: Students take a written paragraph and highlight words that would be stressed, focusing on stressing content English words such as nouns, verbs, adverbs over process words such as articles, prepositions, linking-verbs/modals, and auxiliaries.

Literacy: To be literate, students have to have the ability to use and process printed and written material in a specific affective filter.

Literature Circles: In this activity students form small groups similar to "book clubs" to discuss literature. Roles include: discussion facilitators, passage pickers, illustrators, connectors, summarizers, vocabulary enrichers, travel tracers, investigators, and figurative language finders. ELLs will need to be supported with sentence starters, wordlists, and adapted text as necessary, depending on language level (Noe & Johnson, 1999). For support in starting literature circles see: http://www.litcircles.org/.

Margin Notes: This is a way of adapting text. Teachers, students, or volunteers write key terms, translations of key terms, short native language summaries, text clarifications, or hints for understanding in the margins of a textbook (Echevarria, Vogt, & Short, 2008).

APPENDIX 4

Math Sorts: This sorting activity requires that students classify numbers, equations, geometric shapes, etc. based on given categories. For example, students are given twenty systems of linear equations cards and they have to determine whether each system belongs in the category of parallel lines, perpendicular lines, or neither.

Mix and Match: This activity encourages students to interact with classmates and to practice formal and informal English. To begin, each student is given a card that has information matching another student's card. When the teacher says, "Mix," students stand and walk around the room. When the teacher says, "Match," students find their match by using the sentence stem, "I have _____. Who has _____?"

Mortar Words: Mortar words are general academic words that can be found in textbooks, tests, and conversations across all subject areas. Mortar words hold academic language (i.e., specific technical words/terms) together in a sentence. They include transitional words (i.e., because), signal words (i.e., first or second), and test-specific language (i.e, best represents or based upon.) Mortar words are often abstract, and without a clear definition, so the best way for students to learn these words is by using them. Mortar words allow students to put complex and formal structures together when communicating.

Multiple Representations Card Game: This activity is a variation of the Spoons card game. Depending on the number of cards, students play in groups of 3-5. The objective of the game is to be the first player to get all the representations of a particular math concept.

Multiple Representations Graphic Organizer (MRGO): This is an instructional tool used to illustrate an algebraic situation in multiple representations that could include: pictures, graphs, tables, equations, or verbal descriptions (Echevarria, Vogt, & Short, 2008).

Native Language Brainstorm: This method allows students to think about and list ideas related to a concept in their native language.

Native Language Texts: Native language translations, chapter summaries, word lists, glossaries, or related literature can be used to understand texts from content area classes. Many textbook companies include Spanish language resources with textbook adoption.

Nonlinguistic Representations: Nonlinguistic means of representing knowledge include illustrations, graphic organizers, physical models, and kinesthetic activities. Marzano et al., (2001) and Hill & Flynn, (2006) advocate integrating Total Physical Response (Asher, 1967) with nonlinguistic representations to engage learners in the early stages of language development.

Note-Taking Strategies: Students learn strategies for organizing information presented in lectures and in texts during note-taking. English Language Learners, at the early stages of language development, benefit from Guided Notes (see description above), native language wordlists, summaries, and opportunities to clarify concepts with peers. Strategies include informal outlines, concept webbing, Cornell Note-taking, and combination notes (see descriptions above). Research indicates that students should write more, rather than less, when taking notes. (Marzano et al., 2001). ELLs in pre-production phases can respond to teacher notes through gestures. Those in early production and speech emergent phases can communicate using teacher provided sentence frames (Hill & Flynn, 2006).

Numbered Heads Together: This strategy enables all students, in small groups, a chance to share with the whole class. Each student in a group is assigned a number (1, 2, 3, and 4). When asking questions, the teacher will ask all the Ones to speak first, and then open the discussion to the rest of the class. For the next question, the teacher will ask the Twos to speak, then the Threes, and finally the Fours. The teacher can also randomize which number will speak in which order. When doing numbered heads with English Language Learners, teachers should provide sentence starters for the students (Kagan, 1992).

Oral Scaffolding: This is the process of: teaching academic language explicitly, modeling academic language, providing structured opportunities to use academic language in oral expression, and writing with academic language (Adapted from Gibbons, 2002).

Order It Up Math Puzzle: In this activity, a number sentence or equation is written on a sentence strip. The sentence strip is cut into individual pieces and placed in an envelope. Students work in pairs to determine the correct order of each piece and to come up with the original number sentence/equation (Created by Amy King, Independent Consultant).

Outlines: This traditional note-taking method makes use of Roman numerals, Arabic numerals, and upper/lowercase letters.

Pairs View: When watching a video clip or movie, each pair of students is assigned a role. For example, one partner might be responsible for identifying key dates while another is listing important people and their actions. (Kagan, 1992). This strategy keeps students engaged and focused while they process information.

Paragraph Frames: Incomplete paragraphs provide scaffolds for language development by offering opportunities to develop academic writing and communication skills.

Partner Reading: This strategy for processing text requires two students to read a text. While reading, readers alternate paragraphs, allowing one student to summarize while the other student reads and vice versa. (Meisinger, Schwanenflugel, Bradley, & Stahl 1995).

Peer Editing: During this activity, students review one another's work using a rubric. Research shows that English Language Learners benefit from peer editing when trained using peer response strategies (Berg, 1999).

PERSIAN: This acronym is used to analyze the characteristics of a society. Elements include: Political, Economic, Religious, Social, Intellectual, Artistic, and Near (geography). This framework helps students organize their thinking about the history, geography, economy, and sociology of a country or region.

Personal Dictionary: To engage in this activity, students choose words from the word wall, wordlists, or words encountered in texts. Words are recorded on note cards or in notebooks which become personal dictionaries. Students are encouraged to draw, reflect, or use their native language when writing definitions (Adapted from Echevarria, Vogt, & Short, 2008).

Personal Spelling Guide: On note cards, students record correct spellings of misspelled words from their writing. As the number of cards grows, students can sort the words, based on each word's characteristics. For example, students can generate categories such as: contractions, big words, words with "ie" or "ei," words that are hard to say, words I have never used, etc. Encourage students to look for spelling patterns as they make lists. To assess spelling knowledge, students can choose a number of self-selected words and have a partner quiz them orally.

Perspective-Based Writing: This activity requires students to write from an assigned point of view using specific academic language. For example, students in a social studies class could write from the perspective of Martin Luther King, Jr., explaining his participation in the Montgomery bus boycott to a fellow pastor. As part of this activity, students are given specific words and phrases to integrate into the writing assignment. Students can also write from the point of view of inanimate objects such as rocks, water, molecules, etc. and describe processes from an imaginative perspective. In addition, students can take on the role of an expert within a field: math, science, social studies, or literature, and use the language of the discipline to write about a particular topic. Genre studies can be a particularly helpful way of preparing students for perspective-based writing activities (Seidlitz & Perryman, 2008).

Polya's Problem-Solving Method: This is a four-step model for solving word problems.

- Step 1: Understanding the problem
- Step 2: Devising a plan
- Step 3: Carrying out the plan
- Step 4: Check

APPENDIX 4

Posted Phrases and Stems: Sentence frames posted in clearly visible locations in the classroom give students easy access to functional language during writing tasks. For example, during a lab, the teacher might post the following sentence stems: "How do I record….," "Can you help me gather/mix/measure/identify/list….," "Can you explain what you mean by …?" Sentence stems should be posted in English but can be written in the native language as well.

Prediction Café: This activity is a way for students to participate in mini-discussions about prediction. Pick out important headings, quotations, or captions from a text (about eight quotations for a class of 24) and write them on cards. Have students read/discuss what they think the text might be about or what they think will happen in the text, based on the information on the card. (Note: Even though some students may receive the same card, predictions will vary.) Students should be given frames to facilitate the development of academic language during the activity such as:"__makes me think that..,""I believe ____ because…," etc. (Zwiers, 2008).

Pretest with a Partner: In pairs, students are given a pretest. Students take turns reading the questions, and after each question they try to come to consensus on answers. This activity prepares students for a unit of study (Echevarria, Vogt, & Short, 2008).

Question Answer Relationship (QAR): This is a way of teaching students to analyze the nature of questions they are asked about a text (Rafael, 2004).

Questions are divided into four categories:

+ Right there (found in the text)
+ Think and Search (requires thinking about relationships between ideas in the text)
+ Author and Me (requires making an inference about the text)
+ On My Own (requires reflection on experience and knowledge)

Question the Author (QtA): This is a strategy for deepening the level of thinking about literature (Beck, McKeown, Hamilton, & Kugan, 2013). Instead of staying within the realm of the text, the teacher prompts students to think about the author's purpose. For example:

+ What do you think the author is trying to say?
+ Why do you think the author chose that word or phrase?
+ Would you have chosen a different word or phrase?

Question, Signal, Stem, Share, Assess: This strategy helps students use new academic language during student-student interactions. The teacher asks a question and then asks students to give a signal when they are ready to share their responses with another student. To respond, students must use a particular sentence stem provided by the teacher. Students are then assessed orally or in writing (Seidlitz & Perryman, 2008).

Quick Write: Within a short time period, students are asked to respond in writing to a specific content concept.

Radio Talk Show: Students create a radio talk show about a particular topic. This can be a good opportunity for students to practice using academic language as they take on the role of an expert. It also provides an opportunity for students to identify the differences between formal and informal use of English as they play different roles (Smith & Wilhelm, 2002).

R.A.F.T. (Role/Audience/Format/Topic): This Social Studies writing strategy enables students to write from various points of view (Fisher & Frey, 2004). The letters stand for Role (the perspective the students take; Audience (the individuals the author is addressing); Format (the type of writing that will take place); Topic (the subject).

Read, Write, Pair, Share: This strategy encourages students to share their writing and ideas during interactions. Students read a text, write their thoughts using a sentence starter, pair with another student, and share their writing. Students can also be given suggestions about responding to one another's writing (Fisher et al, 2007).

Reader/Writer/Speaker Response Triads: This is a way of processing text in cooperative groups. To begin, students form groups of three. One student reads the text aloud; one writes the group's reactions or responses to questions about the text, a third reports the answers to the group. After reporting to the group, the students switch roles (Echevarria, Vogt, & Short 2008).

Recasting: For this activity, repeat an English Language Learner's incorrect statement or question correctly. Do not change the meaning or the low-risk environment. Be sure the learner feels comfortable during the interaction. Recasts have been shown to have a positive impact on second language acquisition (Leeman, 2003).

Reciprocal Teaching: Reciprocal teaching requires a student leader to guide the class through the following learning stages: Summarizing, Question Generating, Clarifying, and Predicting. This student-student interaction involves collaboration to create meaning from texts. Palincsar and Brown (1985) and Hill and Flynn (2006) suggest adapting reciprocal teaching for use among English Language Learners by providing vocabulary, modeling language use, and using pictorial representation during the discussion.

Related Literature: Related literature is text that connects and supports subject-area content. These texts can be fiction or nonfiction, in the native language, or in the target language (Echevarria, Vogt, & Short, 2008).

ReQuest: This is a variation of reciprocal teaching (see description above). The teacher asks questions using particular sentence stems after a SSR session (see description below). During the next SSR session, the teacher provides stems for students to use when responding to the text (Manzo, 1969: as cited in Fisher & Frey, 2007).

Retelling: During this activity, students retell a narrative text or summarize an expository text using their own words.

Roundtable: This is a cooperative learning technique in which small groups are given a paper with a category, term, or task listed. The paper is passed around the table and each group member is responsible for writing a characteristic, synonym, step, or task that represents the category, term, or task (Kagan, 1992).

Same Scene Twice: Students perform a skit that involves individuals discussing a given topic. The first time, the individuals are novices who use informal language to discuss the topic. The second time, they are experts who discuss the topic using correct academic terminology and academic English (Adapted from Wilhelm, 2002).

Scanning: Students scan through a text backwards looking for unfamiliar terms. The teacher then provides quick, brief definitions for the terms, giving only the meaning of the word as it appears in context. Marzano et al., (2001) state that "even superficial instruction on words greatly enhances the probability that students will learn the words from context when they encounter them during reading," and that "the effects of vocabulary instruction are even more powerful when the words selected are those that students will most likely encounter when they learn new content."

Sculptorades: Based on one of the tasks in the board game Cranium, this strategy requires each student to use sculpting clay to represent a concept, object, organism, or process. Students can be assigned a broad category or given specific vocabulary terms to model. All students should sculpt at the same time, preferably behind folders. One at a time, each student reveals their sculpture, and the other group members try to determine what the sculpture represents.

Segmental Practice: These listening/discriminating activities help English Language Learners listen for and practice pronouncing individual combinations of syllables. There are several ways to engage in segmental practice. Tongue Twisters and comparisons with native language pronunciations help English Language Learners practice English pronunciation. Using "syllable, storm, say," students brainstorm syllables that begin with a particular sound, e.g., pat, pen, pal, pas, pon, pem, etc. Long and short vowel sounds can be used as well as diphthongs. Students can practice with partners (Celce-Murcia, Brinton & Goodwin, 1996: as cited in Flores, 1998).

Self-Assessment of Levels of Word Knowledge: Students rank their knowledge of new words on the word wall and other word lists using total response signals (see description below) or sentence starters. Responses range from no familiarity with the word to understanding a word well enough to explain it to others. (Diamond & Gutlohn, 2006: as cited in Echevarria, Vogt, & Short, 2008).

Sentence Frames: Incomplete sentences provide the opportunity to scaffold language development structures that help students develop academic language.

Sentence Mark Up: Students use colored pencils to mark texts for cause and effect, opposing thoughts, connecting words, and other features of sentences. This strategy helps students understand the relationship between clauses (Zwiers, 2008).

Sentence Sort: This activity requires students to sort various sentences based on characteristics. The teacher provides the sentences, and the students sort them. In an "open sort," students create the categories; in a "closed sort," teachers create the categories. Sentences can also be taken from a paragraph in a textbook or from class literature.
Possible categories include:

+ Descriptive sentences
+ Complex sentences
+ Simple sentences
+ Sentences connecting ideas
+ Sentences comparing ideas
+ Sentences opposing ideas
+ Sentences with correct usage
+ Sentences with incorrect usage
+ Sentences in formal English
+ Sentences in informal English

Sentence Stems: Incomplete sentences are provided to scaffold the development of specific language structures and to facilitate entry into conversation and writing. For example, "In my opinion…" or "One characteristic of annelids is…"

Signal Words: Signal words determine a text pattern such as generalization, cause and effect, process, sequence, etc. A sample of signal words can be found at: www.nifl.gov/readingprofiles/Signal_Words.pdf

Six-Step Vocabulary Process: This research-based process, developed by Marzano (2004), helps teachers take different steps to build student academic vocabulary. The steps are: Teacher provides a description of a vocabulary word/term. Students restate the description in their own words. Students create a nonlinguistic representation of the word/term. Students periodically do activities that help them add to their knowledge of vocabulary words/terms. Periodically, students are asked to discuss the terms with each other. Periodically, students are involved in games that allow them to "play" with the terms.

SOAPST (Speaker/Occasion/Audience/Purpose/Subject/Tone): This AP writing strategy requires students to address a speaker, occasion, audience, subject, or tone using narrative, persuasive, or analytical writing styles (Wilson, 2009).

Social Language: This is informal language that students use in relationships with peers, friends, and family.

Songs, Poems, Rhymes: Teachers use songs, poems, and rhymes for the purpose of practicing social studies words/terms in the classroom.

Sound Scripting: This is a way for students to mark text showing pauses and stress. Students write a paragraph, enter a paragraph break to show pauses, and use capital and bold letters to show word stress (Powell, 1996).

SQP2RS (Squeepers): This classroom reading strategy trains students to use cognitive/metacognitive strategies to process nonfiction text. The following steps are involved (Echevarria, Vogt, & Short, 2008):

+ Survey: Students scan the visuals, headings, and other text features.
+ Question: Students write a list of questions they might answer while reading.
+ Predict: Students write predictions about what they will learn.
+ Read: Students read the text.

+ Respond: Students revisit their questions and think through responses to reading.

SSR Program (Sustained, Silent Reading Program): This program encourages students to read books of their choice during a silent reading period of 15-20 minutes per day. Pilgreen (2000) defines the eight features of high-quality SSR programs as: access to books, book appeal, conducive reading environment, encouragement to read, non-accountability, distributed reading time, staff training, and follow up activities.

Story Telling: In this activity, students retell narratives in their native language.

Structured Academic Controversy: This is a way of structuring classroom discussion to promote deep thinking and to understand multiple perspectives. Johnson & Johnson (1999) outline these five steps:

+ Organizing Information and Deriving Conclusions
+ Presenting and Advocating Positions
+ Uncertainty Created By Being Challenged By Opposing Views
+ Epistemic Curiosity and Perspective Taking
+ Reconceptualizing, Synthesizing, and Integrating

Structured Conversation: In this activity, student/student interaction is explicitly planned. Students are given sentence frames to begin the conversation as well as specific questions and sentence starters for the purpose of elaboration.

Summarization Frames: This is a way of structuring summaries of content area text. The frames involve specific questions that help students summarize different kinds of texts. Marzano et al. (2001) and Hill and Flynn (2006) discuss seven frames:

+ narrative frame
+ topic restriction frame
+ illustration frame
+ definition frame
+ argumentation frame
+ problem solution frame
+ conversation frame

Supra-segmental Practice: This activity involves pronunciation practice with groups of syllables. Some techniques include: sound scripting, recasting, pronunciation portfolio, and content/function word comparisons (Wennerstrom, 2001).

Systematic Phonics Instruction: This method teaches sound/spelling relationships and how to use those relationships to read. The National Literacy Panel (2006) reported that instruction in phonemic awareness, phonics, and fluency had "clear benefits for language minority students."

T-Chart, Pair, Defend: On a T-Chart, students write evidence to support two opposing points of view. In pairs, students take turns arguing from each point of view.

Taped Text: Recordings of text can be used as a way of adapting text for English Language Learners (Echevarria, Vogt, & Short, 2008).

Think Alouds: Thinking aloud allows teachers to scaffold cognitive and metacognitive thinking by verbalizing the thought process (Bauman, Jones, & Seifert-Kessell, 1993).

Think, Pair, Share: This method encourages student/student interaction. The teacher asks a question and then provides wait time. The students then find a partner and compare their answers. Afterward, selected students share their thoughts with the whole class (Lyman, 1987).

Ticket Out: To get a "Ticket Out" of class, students write a short reflection at the end of a lesson. The reflection includes facts, details, ideas, impressions, opinions, information, and vocabulary from the unit they have just studied. To help students begin writing, a prompt can be offered.

Tiered Questions: In this activity, there are various types of questions for students that are based on individual levels of language development (Hill & Flynn, 2006).

Tiered Response Stems: This activity asks a single question but allows students to choose from a variety of stems to construct responses. When responding, students can use a sentence stem based on their level of language knowledge and proficiency (Seidlitz & Perryman, 2008).

Total Physical Response (TPR): This is a way of teaching that uses gesture and movement to make content comprehensible to ESL newcomers (Asher, 1967).

Total Response Signals (also called Active Response Signals): Total response signals, such as thumbs up/down, white boards, and response cards, can be used by students when responding to questions. Response signals show levels of comprehension instantly.

Unit Study for English Language Learners: This modified approach to Writers' Workshop is advocated by Samway (2006). The steps involve:

- gathering high quality samples of a genre.
- immersion in books.
- sifting between books that students can model and those they can't.
- repetitive immersion/second reading of the books.
- imitating writing techniques found in published writing.
- writing and publishing.
- reflecting and assessing.

Visual Literacy Frames: This is a framework for improving visual literacy focusing on affective, compositional, and critical dimensions of visual information processing (Callow, 2008).

Visuals: Illustrations, graphic organizers, manipulatives, models, and real world objects are used to make content comprehensible for English Language Learners.

Vocabulary Alive: Students memorize a lesson's key vocabulary by applying gestures to each term. The gestures can be assigned by the teacher or by students. Once the gestures are determined, each term and its gesture is introduced by saying, "The word is _____ , and it looks like this _____." (Created by Cristina Ferrari, Brownsville ISD).

Vocabulary Game Shows: Using games like Jeopardy, Pictionary, and Who Wants to be a Millionaire etc., allows students a chance to practice academic vocabulary.

Vocabulary Self-Collection: This is a research-based method of vocabulary instruction involving student collection of words for class study. As students share their lists, they tell: where the word was found, the definition of the word, and why the class should study that particular word (Ruddell & Shearer 2002).

W.I.T. Questioning: This is a questioning strategy that trains students to use three stems to promote elaboration during discussion (Seiditz & Perryman, 2008);

- Why do you think…?
- Is there another…?
- Tell me more about…

Whip Around: This is a way of getting input from all students during a class discussion. To begin, the teacher asks students to write a bulleted list in response to an open-ended question. Students write their responses to the question and then stand up. The teacher calls on students, one at a time, to respond to the question. If students have the same answer as the student who is responding, they cross it off their lists. The teacher continues to call on students for responses, and students continue to cross off answers that are similar. When all answers have been deleted, the students sit down. The activity concludes when all students are seated (Fisher & Frey, 2007).

Word Analysis: In this activity, students study the parts, origins, and structures of words for the purpose of improving spelling skills (Harrington, 1996).

Word Generation: In this activity, students brainstorm words having particular roots. Teachers then have students predict the meaning of the word based on the roots (Echevarria, Vogt, & Short, 2008).

Word, Model, Expand, and Sound Questioning (WMES Questioning): This is a method of differentiating instruction developed by Hill and Flynn (2006). The mnemonic device stands for "Word, Model, Expand, and Sound."

- Word: Teachers work on word selection with pre-production students.
- Model: Teachers model for early production.
- Expand: Teachers expand the written or spoken language of speech emergent students.
- Sound: Teachers help intermediate and advanced fluency students sound "like a book" by working on fluency.

Word Play: In this activity, students manipulate words through various word games designed to increase understanding. Johnson, von Hoff Johnson, & Shlicting (2004) divide word games into eight categories: onomastics (name games), expressions, figures of speech, word associations, word formations, word manipulations, word games, and ambiguities.

Word Sorts: Sorting words based on structure and spelling can improve orthography (Bear & Invernizzi, 2004).

Word Splash: Select key vocabulary words or words connected to a concept and write them for students to see. Tell students you wrote the words in no particular order (called a splash). Have students begin to categorize the words in some logical order. Ask students to choose the words from one category to use in a written paragraph, and then ask them to share it orally with the class.

Word Study Books: In this activity, students organize words in a notebook based on spelling, affixes, and roots (Invernizzi & Hayes 2004).

Word Walls: Word walls are a collection of words posted on a classroom wall used to improve literacy. Not only do they become silent teachers that remind students of words studied in class, but they provide opportunities to have language moments whenever possible. Word walls can be organized by topic, sound, or spelling. The content on word walls should be changed as units of study are completed (Eyraud et al., 2000).

Written Conversation: Using planned language and content, students interact during writing conversation. To complete this activity, students work in pairs as they respond to questions and sentence starters provided by the teacher.

BIBLIOGRAPHY

Allington, R., (2002). *What I've learned about effective reading instruction from a decade of studying exemplary elementary classroom teachers.* Phi Delta Kappan. Retrieved from: http://www.insinc.com/ministryofeducation/20041007/assets/Allington.pdf

Anderson, L. W., Krathwohl, D. R., & Bloom, B. S. (2005). *A Taxonomy for Learning, Teaching, and Assessing.* Longman.

Asher, J. J., & Price, B. S. (1967). The learning strategy of the total physical response: Some age differences. *Child Development,* 1219-1227.

Baker, W., & Boonkit, K. (2004). Learning strategies in reading and writing: EAP contexts. *RELC Journal, 35*(3), 299-328.

Baumann, J. F., Jones, L. A., & Seifert-Kessell, N. (1993). Using think alouds to enhance children's comprehension monitoring abilities. *The Reading Teacher, 47*(3), 184-193.

Beck, I. L., McKeown, M. G., & Kucan, L. (2013). *Bringing Words to Life: Robust Vocabulary Instruction.* Guilford Press.

Berg, E. C. (1999). The effects of trained peer response on ESL students' revision types and writing quality. *Journal of Second Language Writing, 8*(3), 215-241.

Bickel, W.E., & Bickel, D.D. (1986). "Effective Schools, Classrooms, and Instruction: Implications for Special Education." *Exceptional Children, 52*(6) 489-500.

Boulware, B. J., & Crow, M. L. (2008). Using the concept attainment strategy to enhance reading comprehension. *The Reading Teacher, 61*(6), 491-495.

British Broadcasting Corporation News Online (2002, November 20). "Reading Can Bring Social Change." (online article) in Schmoker (2006).

Brown, A. L., Campione, J. C., & Day, J. D. (1981). Learning to learn: On training students to learn from texts. *Educational Researcher, 10*(2), 14-21.

Bruner, J. S. (1973). Organization of early skilled action. *Child Development,* 1-11.

Bruner, J. S., & Kalnins, I. V. (1973). The coordination of visual observation and instrumental behavior in early infancy. *Perception, 2,* 307-314.

Caldwell, J., (1994). "Clickers in the Large Classroom: Current Research and Best-practice Tips." *Journal of Applied Behavioral Analysis.* 27(1), 63-71.

Callow, J. (2008). Show me: Principles for assessing students' visual literacy. *The Reading Teacher, 61*(8), 616-626.

Celce-Murcia, M., Brinton, D. M., & Goodwin, J. M. (Eds.). (1996). Teaching Pronunciation Audio Cassette: A Reference for Teachers of English to Speakers of Other Languages. Cambridge University Press.

Chamot, A. U., & O'Malley, J. M. (1994). "Instructional Approaches and Teaching Procedures." In K. S. Urbschat & R. Pritchard (Eds.), *Kids Come in All Languages: Reading Instruction for ESL Students.* Newark, DE: International Reading Association.

Christle, C. & Schuster, J. (2003). "The Effects of Using Response Cards on Student Participation, Academic Achievement, and On-task Behavior During Whole-class Math Instruction." *Journal of Behavioral Education.* 12(3), 403-406.

Clay, M. (1991). *Becoming Literate: The Construction of Inner Control.* Portsmouth, NH: Heinemann.

Daniels, H., & Steineke, N. (2004). Mini-lessons for Literature Circles.

Diamond, L., & Gutlohn, L. (2006). *Vocabulary Handbook.* Brookes.

Dole, J. A., Duffy, G. G., Roehler, L. R., & Pearson, P. D. (1991). Moving from the old to the new: Research on reading comprehension instruction. *Review of Educational Research, 61*(2), 239-264.

Dutro, S., & Moran, C. (2003). Rethinking English language instruction: An architectural approach. *English Learners: Reaching the Highest Level of English Literacy,* 227-258.

Duffy, G. (2002). "The Case for Direct Explanation of Strategies." In C.C. Block & M. Pressley (Eds..) in (Echevarria, J., Vogt, M., & Short, D.) *Comprehension Instruction: Research-based Best Practices.* New York, NY: Guilford Press.

Echevarria, J., Vogt, M., & Short, D., (2008). *Making Content Comprehensible for English Learners, The SIOP Model.* Boston, MA: Pearson Education, Inc.

Elbow, P. (1998). *Writing Without Teachers.* Oxford University Press.

Eyraud, K., Giles, G., Koenig, S., & Stoller, F. L. (2000). The Word Wall Approach: Promoting L2 Vocabulary Learning. In *English Teaching Forum Online* (Vol. 38, No. 3). http:// exchanges. state. gov/forum/.

Fisher, D., & Frey, N. (2007). Implementing a schoolwide literacy framework: Improving achievement in an urban elementary school. *The Reading Teacher, 61*(1), 32-43.

Fisher, D., Frey, N., Fearn, L., Farnan, N., & Petersen, F. (2004). Increasing Writing Achievement in an Urban Middle School. *Middle School Journal, 36*(2), 21-26.

Florez, M. C. (1998). *Improving adult ESL learners' pronunciation skills.* ERIC, National Clearinghouse for ESL Literacy Education.

Fountas, I. & Pinnell, G. (2001). *Guiding Readers and Writers Grades 3-6: Teaching Comprehension, Genre, and Content Literacy.* Portsmouth, NH: Heinemann.

Gagnon, J. & Maccini, P. (2000). "Best Practices for Teaching Mathematics to Secondary Students with Special Needs: Implications from Teacher Perceptions and a Review of the Literature." *Focus on Exceptional Children, 32* (5), 1-22.

Gardner, R. III, Hewad, W., & Grossi, T., (1996). "Effects of Response Cards on Student Participation and Academic Achievement: A Systematic Replication with Inner-City Students during Whole Class Science Instruction." *Journal of Applied Behavior Analysis.* 29(3), 403-406.

Geva, E. (2006). "Second-Language Oral Proficiency and Second-Language Literacy." In D. August & T. Shanahan (Eds.), *Developing Literacy in Second-language Learners: Report of the National Literacy Panel on Language Minority Children and Youth.* Mahwah, NJ: Lawrence Earlbaum Associates.

Gibbons, P. (2002). *Scaffolding Language, Scaffolding Learning: Teaching Second Language Learners In The Mainstream Classroom.* Portsmouth, NH: Heinemann.

Goldenberg, C. (1992). Instructional conversations: Promoting comprehension through discussion. *The Reading Teacher, 46*(4), 316-326.

Graff, G. (2003). *Clueless in Academe.* New Haven, CT: Yale University Press.

Guzetti, B.J., Snyder, T.E., & Glass, G.V. (1993). "Promoting Conceptual Change in Science: A Comparative Meta-analysis of Instructional Interventions from Reading Education and Science Education." *Reading Research Quarterly, 28*(2), 117-155.

Harrington, M. J. (1996). Basic Instruction in Word Analysis Skills to Improve Spelling Competence. *Education, (117)*1

Head, M. H., Readence, J. E., & Buss, R. R. (1989). An examination of summary writing as a measure of reading comprehension. *Literacy Research and Instruction, 28*(4), 1-11.

Hill, J., & Flynn, K. (2006). *Classroom Instruction that Works with English Language Learners.* Alexandria, VA: Association for Supervision and Curriculum Development.

Invernizzi, M., & Hayes, L. (2004). Developmental spelling research: A systematic imperative. *Reading Research Quarterly, 39*(2), 216-228.

Jenkins, J., Stein, M., & Wysocki, K. (1984). Learning Vocabulary Through Reading. *American Education Research Journal, 21* (4), 767-787.

Jensen, E. (2005). *Teaching with the Brain in Mind (2nd Ed.).* Alexandria, VA: Association for Supervision and Curriculum Development.

BIBLIOGRAPHY

Johnson, D., Maruyama, G., Johnson, R., Nelson, D., and Skon, L. (1981). "Effects of Cooperative, Competitive, and Individualistic Goal Structures on Achievement: A Meta-analysis." *Psychological Bulletin, 89* (1), 47-62.

Johnson, D.W., & Johnson, R.T. (1999). *Learning Together and Alone: Cooperative, Competitive, and Individualistic Learning.* Boston, MA: Allyn & Bacon.

Johnson, D. W., & Johnson, R. T. (1999). Making cooperative learning work. *Theory into practice, 38*(2), 67-73.

Kagan, S., (1992). *Cooperative Learning.* San Juan Capistrano, CA: Kagan Cooperative Learning.

Kagan, S. (1995). We can talk: Cooperative learning in the elementary ESL classroom (ERIC Digest). *Washington, DC: ERIC Clearinghouse on Languages and Linguistics (May, 1995).*

Krashen, S. (1982). *Principles and Practice in Second Language Acquisition* (pp. 65-78). Pergamon: Oxford.

LeDoux, J. (December 20, 1993). "Emotional Memory Systems in the Brain." *Behavioral Brain Research 58* (1-2), 69-79.

Leeman, J. (2003). Recasts and second language development. *Studies in Second Language Acquisition, 25*(01), 37-63.

Lipson, M., & Wixson, K. (2008). *Assessment and Instruction of Reading and Writing Difficulties: An Interactive Approach (3rd Ed.).* New York , NY: Longman.

Lyman, F. (1987). Think-Pair-Share. Unpublished University of Maryland paper.

Macon, J. M., Bewell, D., and Vogt, M. (1991). *Responses to Literature.* Newark, DE: IRA.

Manzo, A. V. (1969). The request procedure. *Journal of Reading, 13*(2), 123-163.

Marzano, R. J. (2004). *Building Background Knowledge for Academic Achievement: Research on What Works in Schools.* ASCD.

Marzano, R., Pickering, D., & Pollock, J. (2001). *Research-based Strategies for Increasing Student Achievement. Classroom Instruction That Works.* Alexandria, VA: Association for Supervision and Curriculum Development.

Mayer, R. E. (2004). Should there be a three-strikes rule against pure discovery learning?. *American Psychologist, 59*(1), 14.

McDougall, D. & Cordeiro, P. (1992). "Effects of Random Questioning Expectations on Education Majors' Preparedness for Lecture and Discussion." *College Student Journal, 26* (2), 193-198.

McLaughlin, M. (2003). *Guided Comprehension in the Primary Grades.* Newark, DE: International Reading Association.

Meyen, E., Vergason, G. & Whelan, R. (1996). *Strategies for Teaching Exceptional Children in Inclusive Settings.* Denver, CO: Love.

Meisinger, E. B., Schwanenflugel, P. J., Bradley, B. A., & Stahl, S. A. (2004). Interaction quality during partner reading. *Journal of Literacy Research, 36*(2), 111-140.

National Institute of Child Health and Human Development. (2000). Teaching Children to Read: An Evidence-Based Assessment of the Scientific Research Literature on Reading and Its Implications for Reading Instruction: Reports of the Sub-groups. (Report of the National Reading Panel, NIH, 00-4754. Washington, DC: US Government Printing Office.

Noe, K. L. S., & Johnson, N. J. (1999). *Getting Started with Literature Circles. The Bill Harp Professional Teachers Library Series.* Christopher-Gordon Publishers, Inc., 1502 Providence Highway, Suite 12, Norwood, MA 02062.

Novak, J. D. (1995). Concept mapping: A strategy for organizing knowledge. *Learning Science in the Schools: Research Reforming Practice,* 229-245.

Ogle, D. M. (1986). KWL: A teaching model that develops active reading of expository text. *The Reading Teacher, 39*(6), 564-570.

Pauk, W. (2013). How to study in college. Cengage Learning.

Pilgreen, J. L. (2000). *The SS Handbook: How to Organize and Manage a Sustained Silent Reading Program*. Portsmouth, NH: Boynton/Cook Publishers.

Rose, M. (1989). *Lives on the Boundary*. New York , NY: Viking Penguin.

Ruddell, M. R., & Shearer, B. A. (2002)." Extraordinary,'''' Tremendous,'''' Exhilarating'''' Magnificent": Middle School at-Risk Students Become Avid Word Learners with the Vocabulary Self-Collection Strategy (VSS). *Journal of Adolescent & Adult Literacy, 45(5)*, 352-363.

Samway, K. D. (2006). *When English Language Learners Write* (Vol. 9). Portsmouth, NH: Heinemann.

Schmoker, M., (2006). *Results Now*. Alexandria, VA: Association for Supervision and Curriculum Development.

Seidlitz, J., & Perryman, B. (2008). Seven steps to building an interactive classroom: Engaging all students in academic conversation.

Smith, M. W., & Wilhelm, J. D. (2002). *"Reading Don't Fix No Chevys": Literacy in the Lives of Young Men*. Heinemann, 361 Hanover Street, Portsmouth, NH 03801-3912.

Snow, C. E.; Griffin, P. & Burns, M. S. (2005). *Knowledge to Support the Teaching of Reading: Preparing Teachers for a Changing World*. San Francisco, CA: Jossey-Bass.

Stahl, S.A., & Fairbanks, M.M. (1986). "The Effects of Vocabulary Instruction: A Model-based Meta-analysis." *Review of Educational Research, 56(1)*, 72-110.

Sweller, J., Kirschner, P. A., & Clark, R. E. (2007). Why minimally guided teaching techniques do not work: A reply to commentaries. *Educational Psychologist, 42(2)*, 115-121.

Taylor, W. L. (1953)." Cloze procedure": a new tool for measuring readability. *Journalism Quarterly*.

Thornberry, T. P. (2005). Explaining multiple patterns of offending across the life course and across generations. *The Annals of the American Academy of Political and Social Science, 602(1)*, 156-195.

Vail, N. J., & Papenfuss, J. F. (2000). *Daily Oral Language: Teacher's Manual. Grade 7*. Great Source Education Group.

Vogt, M., & Nagano, P. (2003)."Turn It on with Light Bulb Reading! Sound-Switching Strategies for Struggling Readers." *Reading Teacher, 57(3)*, 214-221.

Weaver, C. (1996). *Teaching Grammar in Context*. Boynton/Cook Publishers, Inc., 361 Hanover Street, Portsmouth, NH 03801-3912.

Wennerstrom, A. (2001). *The Music of Everyday Speech: Prosody and Discourse Analysis*. Oxford University Press.

White, T. G., Sowell, J., & Yanagihara, A. (1989). Teaching elementary students to use word-part clues. *The Reading Teacher, 42(4)*, 302-308

Wiggins, G. & McTighe, J. (1998). *Understanding by Design, (2nd Ed.)*. Alexandria, VA: Association for Supervision and Curriculum Development.

Zwiers, J. (2008). *Building Academic Language*. Newark, DE: Jossey-Bass/International Reading Association.

SEIDLITZ PRODUCT ORDER FORM

Three ways to order

- **FAX** completed order form with payment information to **(949) 481-3864**
- **PHONE** order information to **(210) 315-7119**
- **ORDER ONLINE** at **www.seidlitzeducation.com**

Pricing, specifications, and availability subject to change without notice.

PRODUCT	PRICE	QUANTITY	TOTAL
NEW! Talk Read Talk Write: A Practical Approach to Learning in the Secondary Classroom	$29.95		
NEW! ELLs in Texas: What Administrators Need to Know	$29.95		
NEW! Vocabulary Now! 44 Strategies All Teachers Can Use	$29.95		
Diverse Learner Flip Book	$26.95		
ELPS Flip Book	$19.95		
Academic Language Cards and Activity Booklet, ENGLISH	$19.95		
Academic Language Cards, SPANISH	$9.95		
Sheltered Instruction Plus	$19.95		
RTI for ELLs Fold-Out	$16.95		
7 Steps to a Language-Rich Interactive Classroom	$29.95		
7 Pasos para crear un aula interactiva y rica en lenguaje SPANISH	$29.95		
Language & Literacy for ELLs Workbook	$29.95		
Language & Literacy for ELLs Handbbook	$29.95		
38 Great Academic Language Builders	$24.95		
An Exemplary Disciplinary Alternative Education Program (DAEP) Handbook with CD-ROM	$29.95		
Navigating the ELPS: Using the Standards to Improve Instruction for English Learners	$24.95		
Navigating the ELPS: Math	$29.95		
Navigating the ELPS: Science	$29.95		
Navigating the ELPS: Social Studies	$29.95		
Navigating the ELPS: Language Arts and Reading	$34.95		
'Instead Of I Don't Know' Poster, Elementary ENGLISH ☐ Elementary ☐ Secondary	$9.95		
'Instead Of I Don't Know' Poster, Elementary SPANISH (Elementary only)	$9.95		
'Please Speak In Complete Sentences' Poster ENGLISH	$9.95		
'Please Speak In Complete Sentences' Poster SPANISH	$9.95		

SHIPPING $14.95 for 1-15 items, plus $1.05 each per additional items over 15.
5-7 business days to ship. If needed sooner please call for rates.
TAX EXEMPT? please fax a copy of your certificate along with order.

DISCOUNT	
SHIPPING	
TAX	
TOTAL	

NAME

SHIPPING ADDRESS   CITY   STATE, ZIP

PHONE NUMBER   EMAIL ADDRESS

TO ORDER BY FAX
to **(949)481-3864**
please complete
credit card info *or*
attach purchase order

☐ Visa ☐ MasterCard ☐ Discover ☐ AMEX

CC# _____ Exp. Date: _____

Signature _____

☐ **Purchase Order attached**
please make
P.O. out to
Seidlitz Education

For information about Seidlitz Education products
and professional development, please contact us at

(210) 315-7119 | kathy@johnseidlitz.com
56 Via Regalo, San Clemente, CA 92673
www.seidlitzeducation.com

Giving kids the
gift of **academic
language.™**

Seidlitz
EDUCATION

REV033114